Into the Music of the World: Living Life Mindfully

To meg
— a fellow
spiritual
traveller —
Marty

Martin Lumpkin

ISBN: 1503015920
ISBN 13: 9781503015920
Library of Congress Control Number: 2014919614
CreateSpace Independent Publishing Platform
North Charleston, South Carolina

*For Janet
the love of my life,
the music in my life.*

*Who can explain
what makes us us?*

*Thank you for all
our duets
played and yet to play.*

There is another world, but it is inside this one.

W. B. Yeats

After silence, that which comes nearest to
expressing the inexpressible is music.
Music is what feelings sound like.

Aldous Huxley

Contents

Introduction

There are many books on mindfulness these days. And I celebrate that. Why one more? If my book deserves your attention, it will be because its language offers a fresh sense of mindfulness and piques your passion to pursue it in your life. I wrote the book doing my best to jettison jargon. For as a topic becomes popular – like mindfulness – there is a tendency for language to get lazy as it settles into commonly used words. I take much of my inspiration for a new strain of writing from Jon Kabat-Zinn and Saki Santorelli, originators of what is arguably the prime mover of mindfulness in popular culture today: Mindfulness Based Stress Reduction. I also take inspiration from the vivid, poetic writings of Thoreau, Emerson, Alan Watts, Aldous Huxley, Abraham Maslow, and Carl Rogers. Along with a variety of Buddhist writers, this is my mindfulness gang.

I would like to say a word about the writing in this book. I want the reading of its pages to be a mindfulness practice. To do this, I tried to bring a sense of the music and poetry of mindfulness forward. I also kept distilling the sentences so that brevity worked in favor of psychic weight. The more condensed the writing became, the more deeply one might take in its carefully chosen words and images. The risk is that more could be elaborated about most topics. But if I say more, that leaves less for you to intuit and find in the depths of your own responses.

There are seven chapters and two special sections. The chapters move you through surprising ways mindfulness shows up in our lives through its benefits and the variety of everyday ways mindfulness enriches us and raises living to a higher octave. There is then a section on mindfulness and suffering or how mindfulness helps to liberate us from our own ways of creating stress. A little piece on spiritual life discloses the thread of mindfulness that is often unseen in the multicolored, patchwork quilt of religions. For those interested in beginning formal mindfulness meditation practice, there is an introduction to a series of methods, each a complement to the other as well as a primary practice in itself. And finally, there is a section of suggestions to further you mindfulness studies. Unless stated otherwise, the poems are my own.

Please consider this book as a companion, accompanying you on your exploration of mindfulness. You hold in your eyes a kind of sheet music on mindfulness. It seems to me I was born in the poetry of silent music, brusquely schooled in prose, and ever after struggled to lift its heavy lid to find the music again. I lift the baton. Let's begin.

One

The Discovery Under Our Noses

Stumbling into Mindfulness

Years ago, I went walking across the campus of Texas Tech University a little after noon. I was dispirited, lonely, worried about my abilities as a graduate student. I was chewing and chewing the cud of compulsive thoughts. Even though I could not think my way through this mire, thinking is what I did, tumbling thoughts like wet-heavy clothes in a dryer. I was ruminating over the past, obsessing over the feared future, lecturing myself with critiques and instructions.

Then something strange happened. Perhaps a moment of sheer fatigue, who knows? But the mental machinery just stopped. And in the reprieve, I looked up and around for a moment. Something shifted inside me. I saw and heard what was around me. A scattering of students made their way home or to class. The campus was lit and crisply itself. I was in a field of movement of bright clarity and quietly astonishing joy. I was but part of a unified swirl of sky, buildings, walkers, light. It lasted for about 10 minutes before I started to think about and analyze it. And though the experience left, I was left with its atmosphere and a lighter mood.

Without knowing it, I had stumbled into a state of pure mindfulness.

For a few moments, I felt myself inside the music of the world.

Then the door shut. I began to struggle to find my way back to that *world inside this one*. It seemed the more I read, the harder I tried, the more it eluded me. Years later I went to my first meditation retreat. While shifts into mindfulness can happen by accident, I came to realize that such doors usually open by degrees through patient practice.

On Our Two Worlds:
To Be or Not To Be,
To Contact or Control?

A Little Greek Tale

Narcissus spurned them,
those who loved him,
leaving one an echo of her former self.
His Nemesis nailed him for this
and gave a curse that looked like a blessing.
Seeing his reflection in a forest pond,
Narcissus could not take his eyes away,
would not take his eyes away,
and wasting away, wasted away
before what he could not have,
unable to wake from the dream of self.

At first, I walked across that campus, Narcissus entranced. Then for a time, Narcissus fell into that pond, becoming the pond itself, reflecting all around me without the heavy me. I glimpsed the possibility of simple, profound pond awareness. The curse of control was lifted for contact.

How our usual selves are like Narcissus! This self values control. It sees the world for its own use and seeks ways to grasp and possess what it wants or ways to escape what threatens. The floating image of I-me-mine screens and filters what is seen in the world. It demands love, success, and security. Underneath it all, this self continually checks and polishes its image. Yet there is unease lurking below: a kind of claustrophobic feeling perhaps. It is a feeling of a treasured room that is now too small. Narcissus creates an imaginary world he then lives in. It is the source of most all of our suffering.

Yet there is another world inside that one. Like the reflecting pond, it is that natural part of us that is simply open without judgments. It can only reflect present moment experiences in a vital sense that Now is where life is lived. It is consciousness without self-consciousness. It is filled with gratitude to be – to be alive.

Mindfulness is awakened attention. Without a self-image to fret over, it is luminous, clear, and free. It is like that moment of morning waking out of a dream. I am amazed to be born into *this* life again *this* day.

Mindfulness comes in degrees. Sometimes it is a complete and pure absorption in the present. But mostly it is small shifts toward freedom from the fretting self – times of being in that self but not completely of it. And this is a shift that can be learned. If we can fall asleep, we can also wake up.

❦

The following poem arose as a way to tag a moment of mindfulness on a quiet lake in Maine one summer. Perhaps you know such moments. Resting from paddling a canoe, I sat back and floated on near breeze-less waters. Little cries suddenly sounded, like questions floating in the sunlit air. There was nothing but the lifting of the boat and the lilting vocals of the loons. Later, when writing of this experience, I felt the loons as something vulnerable in me. Something flying and landing was soft and fragile, yet the very soul of me. This something could be outshouted by geese, shot at and scattered into flight, but also held by the supporting waters of a lake home. This home is a place within, like mindfulness itself, beyond the noise of the world we have too often taken in.

Lake Loons

Be quiet.
Be so still
your body breathes
in the space left by
the honking geese of thoughts
now fading over the horizon.
Be so still
the feeling (that small tightness)
of yourself dissolves into
the waters of the host of things
around you now
moving, standing, sounding, breathing. Be so still you are quietly held
in this Holding always under the noise of the world piercing our bodies,
silencing and scattering the loons from their lake.
Be so very quiet
and still
that the shocks
fall from your body
like impotent arrows
as you turn and wing
back to the lake
you left and

light.

৶৵৵

On Marion's Discovery of her Mindful Self

Though modern day mindfulness was lifted from meditation traditions, there were those who also stumbled onto it. May I tell you about one pioneer who discovered on her own this lake within?

Marion Milner, a Londoner born in 1900, set out on a quest when she was a fresh, young adult. She recorded it in a journal, published as *A Life of One's Own*. The seven-year exploration used a compass of one question: What kinds of experience made me happy? Her method was to select and note moments in her life that were particularly alive, then seeing if some pattern ran through them. It is a fascinating and human book not based on other's thoughts or studies. Her findings surprised her.

What Marion had told herself she wanted to make her happy (job success, pleasing people, social standing, even romance) did not produce anything lasting – except more stressful striving.

> "I tried to learn, not from my reason but from
> my senses. But as soon as I began to study my
> perception, to look at my own experience, I
> found that there were different ways of perceiving
> and that the different ways provided me with
> different facts. There was a narrow focus which
> meant seeing life as if from blinkers and with the
> center of awareness in my head; and there was a
> wide focus which meant knowing with the whole
> body, a way of looking which quite altered my
> perception of whatever I saw…it was the wide
> focus that made me happy."

Marion found that there is a monkey in the machinery of clear, open perception. It was Narcissus: critical, striving, ever-judging, always commenting self. Voices in our head separate us from our direct experience and impose a screen of fantasies between us and the world. She called it "blind thinking." It is what we today recognize from cognitive therapists as automatic thinking. It is reactive, judgmental, opinionated, and authoritarian. It warns: Don't make a fool of yourself! It criticizes: How stupid can you be? It blames: He is so selfish! It commands: Don't show emotion or you'll look weak! These thoughts arise in a flash yet bear the weight of seeming like the truth. Emotional reactions come tumbling and rumbling after them.

Another aspect of this blind thinking: It is busy writing the story of our lives. We become the main character in a story shaped by our hopes, disappointments, and desires. Events are mentally written into this story line and given meaning as part of our story. Much of life is spent tuning into this story as it is being related in our heads.

"What does breaking out of blind thinking look like?" -- wondered Marion.

> 'One day I was idly watching some gulls as they soared high overhead. I was not interested, for I recognized them as "just gulls," and vaguely watched first one and then another. Then all at once something seemed to have opened. My idle boredom with the familiar became a deep-breathing peace and delight, and my whole attention was gripped by the pattern and rhythm of their flight, their slow sailing which had become a quiet dance."

Two

Fruits of Mindfulness

When you walk up to mindfulness and ask what you want, what do you say? You may begin with small things. Less stress, perhaps. You want to be more at ease in your own skin. Then it dawns on you. Slowly, it is sensed at first. These seeds grow into something large and transformative, an oak with ever-spreading limbs. Peace is far deeper than surface relaxation. Aliveness is more electric than momentary excitement. The roots of connection enfold and hold your life in something larger than social networks. A new integrity grows from your capacity to touch the self beyond your mind. Beauty and harmony outpace competition and acquisitions. Outpouring intimacy dwarfs "getting the love you want."

Here are a few fruits of mindfulness practice some commonly notice. You come to feel:

1. More intensely alive in your senses and body
2. Clarity of concentration and focus

3. Enhanced relishing of simple present experiences like music, food, movement, sun and wind
4. Greater calm from spotting stressful reactions beginning to swell and quietly choosing to let them go
5. Stronger, more empathic connections with others
6. Sharpened intuition and synthesis of ideas and solutions
7. Ease: Overall less strain and pressure
8. Better at being with and digesting profound or intense emotional experiences, often left undigested in the past
9. A sense of being more than just my self, a sense of some vital and indefinable Whole giving all within it wordless meaning and support
10. A gratuitous, quiet joy and gratitude
11. An intimacy of touch in the way heart and perception merge
12. A desire for a way of living that is no longer rushed and crowded: a way more inwardly rich than outwardly accumulating

These and other fruits grow in the garden tilled by simple, sustained practice.

Three

The Dust We Throw in Our Own Eyes

Don't Think! See!
Don't Leave! Stay!
Don't Distance! Touch!

Mindful moments occur naturally. Time slows. The present fills your cup to the brim. You are transported for a while. Can mindfulness be more than a happy series of accidents?

Yes.

If we are willing to see and choose against the strong undertows of habit and automatic reactions. If we invest time in getting to know what blocks our natural draw toward mindfulness. If we are willing to sharply sense the difference between our usual thoughts and fantasies and the clear state of attention to what is happening here and now. It is like having drunk colored, flavored liquid all our lives and forgetting the bright, lucid taste of pure spring water.

Blocks and Undertows

Marion Milner called one block to mindfulness "blind thinking." But there are other blocks and undertows we rarely notice. These mental modes feel so normal we rarely stand back to see them. Yet they take up most of our time, energy, and mental space. You might feel them as ocean currents below the surface pulling you out to sea. Here are two other such undertows: goal-fixation and self-narrating.

Goal-fixation often goes under the names of goal-setting, planning, and pursuing results. While there is nothing wrong with such pursuits, fixation goes to an extreme. Our eye is too much on the outcome and too little on present experience. We are perceptually blind and inflexibly driven. We are steps ahead of ourselves. We freeze the picture of the goal and lose the fluidity of the current situation.

Goal-fixation is a blinder often defeating its own purpose. You are playing golf and insisting on the perfect shot. The strain sends the shot into the sand pit. You are driven by a list of things to do during the day, speedily trying to check off each thing. Little off the list is seen; mistakes are made in the rush. You are in a meeting mostly hearing your own reactive thoughts. You realize later you missed new information. Each of these blinders stokes stress and tension. Frustration and impatience follow from reality's refusal to comply with our demands.

How much of your day is taken up with goal-fixations? At the end of the day, is there a blur of experiences not fully felt through? How much of your mental time is taken with tasks or problems? How much time goes to strained focusing that rarely gets loosened?

Self-narrating is more an inwardly focused and subtle activity. It is capable of totally consuming our attention or dividing our attention between it and something else going on. James Joyce in *Dubliners* has written about a character named Duffy in this way: "He lived a little distance from his body... He had an odd autobiographical habit which led him to compose in his mind from time to time a short sentence about himself..." Sound familiar? It should. This, and more, is what we are doing so much of the time. We dignify it as "just thinking." But it is more like a daydream full of reverie, rumination, and rummaging. It is the ongoing story of our self, a self gazing at reflections of his or her image.

Let us extend Duffy's comment to say more: He lived apart from and dimly aware of body and surrounds. Instead, he sometimes watched and sometimes took an active part in imaginary elaborations of some matter of presumed urgency and importance. Even when the spell of this imaginary film was broken by something, he quickly returned to it throughout his day. As things happened, he would wrap those events in this imaginary world. This way of living and engaging daily life was so natural and habitual he was largely unaware of it.

Woody Allen has a great image for the self-narrating mind. The center of his movie *The Purple Rose of Cairo* takes place in a movie theatre. The heroine of the movie watches with rapt attention a romantic movie. Then at one point, she gets up and enters the movie as one of its characters. It is easy to smile at Allen's antics. But we realize that this is what we do in *our* mental movies. Sometimes we are a passive spectator entranced in the film. Sometimes we enter the film as we try to shape its direction. Sound crazy? What about times you enter a memory of a conversation with someone and then join in as you try to change the way it went?

When you start to quietly pause and look inward, you may be surprised and dismayed by the consuming power of this self-narrating film. Sometimes it is a voice talking, sometimes a self talking to self about itself, sometimes memory or fanciful associations, and sometimes a fantasy involving past or future. When our attention is divided between the film and this present reality, we – like Duffy – are out of touch. The addictive pull of this self-narrating takes much energy and spins many emotions.

Mindfulness may sound simple but it is up against strong and insistent competitors. Milner's blind thinking is always quick to judge. Goal-fixation keeps attention mentally pinned to a desired result. And self-narration spins its web of inner drama. Like the heroine in *The Purple Rose of Cairo*, we live more in the theatres of our thoughts and fantasies than in the daylight outside. No wonder mindfulness depends upon conscious practices! And it takes such patient practice to wake from the judge's verdicts, the strain for rewards, the inner dream. The simple act of attention is not so simple after all.

Now let us turn to perspectives and principles behind mindful practices. From there, we will unfold informal ways of practice. We practice informally when we catch and expand moments in our days into mindful experiences. In a special section at the end of the book, we will more deeply explore formal methods of cultivating this clear and open mind.

The Perspective of Presence

Being mindfully present means feeling the center of gravity in the newly minted Now. It is life seen and felt outside the inner movie theatre. This is such a difference between a reality sensed in silent perception and a reality shaped by words and imagination. The tree you see outside the window in its *tree-ness* is not the familiar elm that is always there.

As we move toward describing the principles of mindfulness, keep a few approaches in your pocket. We might call these the "be-attitudes." First, try suspending strong judgments and expectations. Keep loose and curious. Play rather than tensely work at being mindful. Second, be kind, gentle, and patient toward yourself. You will falter and backslide -- that's all part of the process. Third, let go of control needs. Get used to allowing all sorts of feelings and experiences to be there without the compulsion to avoid or change them. Mindfulness has a paradoxical nature. Growth and change occur when strained efforts to change are released.

Four

Principles Behind the Practices of Mindfulness

Practices are knitted by principles. If you grasp the principles, the practices not only make sense but they help you appreciate what they are developing in you.

Mindfulness lives in the realm of direct perception outside mental labels, explanations, commentary, and judgments. Primary experience is wordless. Aldous Huxley writes in his essay "Knowledge and Understanding": "Knowledge is acquired when we succeed in fitting a new experience into the system of concepts based upon old experiences. Understanding comes when we liberate ourselves from the old and so make possible a direct, unmediated contact with the new, the mystery, moment by moment, of our existence." Rediscovery of vital, direct experience as a source of knowing: that is the mission of mindfulness. And that is the basic principle.

So how did Marion develop her wide perceiving of sea gulls?

Though I list various principles below, they all begin with a profoundly simple act. You observe without comment your present experience. You pause, step back and become intent to just be present to what you see, hear, feel in your body -- even what is going through your mind.

This kind of observing is done with what is called *beginner's mind*. In the mind of the beginner, there is fresh perceiving and curiosity. There is a kind of excitement of being in new, no longer taken-for-granted experiences. Observing has the quality of knowing that everything arising in your world now is unforeseen and unforeseeable. The present is no longer a blur as you go traveling in your thoughts and fantasies. It is felt as the central reality. Observing is often flush with feeling. Here is how the poet Walt Whitman describes it in "Song of Myself."

"Apart from the pulling and hauling stands
I am."

"Looking with side-curved head curious what
will come next. Both in and out of the game
and watching and wondering at it."

This is a good place to pause before going on. Do you
have some sense of this natural way of observing? What
is it like to take a moment and step back right now?
Without bias or thought, can you simply take in your
sensations – whatever they are – in your body? Can
your hear sounds without having to talk to yourself about
them? What is it like to just open and see what is
around you with no other desire but to see?

The act of present observation can be grown. Good news! The principles below reveal ways growth works for evoking and deepening mindfulness in our living:

1. Recognizing mindful from unmindful states. You directly sense the difference between your habitual mode of mind and the feel of the mindful mode.

    This is not unlike learning a dance by feel than by foot charts. You see the difference between thoughts, feelings, sensations – and the quiet act of observing. You no longer fuse all these together into one heap.

2. Centering yourself in open awareness rather than narrowly focusing on the contents of your mind.

    This is Milner's wide perceiving in which your reading this sentence is surrounded by a space that includes sensations of sitting, a sense of the whole page, sensations in the periphery of your vision, breath and body feelings...

3. Becoming embodied. You foster a grounded sense of total body sensations rather than live primarily from the center of your head.

    Remember Mr. Duffy? We want to shift from Duffy-mind to a sense of being in a living in a body full of changing sensations and movements.

4. Feeling the realness and vividness of the present.

    On a train, a passenger looks dreamily out a window at the blur of landscapes. He is thinking about his destination and his desire to leave the past. Another passenger looks with intense interest at the people in the car, then turns to let the landscapes fill his eyes.

5. Moving from tolerance to acceptance to intimacy as ways of relating to immediate experience.

    In sitting meditation, for example, I may begin with simply tolerating the unfamiliar contact with feelings and sensations. Later, I move into an easier acceptance as I no longer fight or resist being in the moment. Finally, I feel intimacy with what I experience...a kind of heartfelt touch as my attention, like a hummingbird draws the juice of the experience.

6. Making conscious choices. Most of our choices are not choices at all. They are reactions barely noticed. They are blurs of habit or impulse. Making mindful choices means seeing choices, options, and outcomes of choosing. It is also the feeling of choice in the making.

    Whew! Sounds complicated? It isn't, really. Mindfulness takes care of that. You will spot times an old reaction rises and starts to take over.

Say, getting angry at the woman who just spilled her many coupons on the floor in front of you in line at the grocery store. Just as you feel your face begin to flush and your heart speeding up, you pause. You silently ask if this is worth the anger and all the inner drama inside your head in its wake. You decide no. And just like that, you unhook and the red tide recedes. You choose calm over agitation.

7. Letting go and being led as you find yourself carried, like a raft in a mountain river or sailboat on a light-winded lake. You are led by the spontaneity of the experience that is newly unfolding. Even choices arise as natural occurrences in this stream. The little self is no longer in full command.

He released the effort of thinking ahead of what to say. He put the notes of his talk aside. He looked at the audience. Then, as if making the talk to himself, he spoke as the subject of his talk rolled out before him. He was both speaker and spectator.

These principles thicken the soup of mindfulness.

Finding (or tuning into) your current state of mind, you simply observe what your mind and emotions are up to. Taken a little further, you shift to being in your awareness rather than absorbed in your mental commenting, self talk, fantasies. Mental activity is allowed to go on; it just no longer highjacks your attention. It is like the difference between being lost in a movie and being aware you are watching a movie.

Then there is centering or settling into the state of mindfulness. A kind of stabilizing is taking place. Once a period of centering occurs, you let go of trying to force or control the experience. Expectations and striving cease. Finding, shifting, centering, and letting go strengthen your power over time to stay in mindfulness.

A Mindful Pause: What does mindful shifting feel like? Lifting your eyes from the page, let in the wider visual field. Float around in it. Sense the whole scene. Then feel for a moment what is going on in your body. Do you notice certain parts of the body, or tense areas, the sensation of sitting on something? Now include your breath. Feel it moving across the sensitive borders of your nostrils. Notice that you are opening your attention wider and wider: first the visual field, then adding your body sensations. Finally, expand to the feeling of breathing. Even though thoughts arise and go, you can experience centering primarily in this larger field of happenings. In this simple exercise, you find, shift, and center for a while in being mindful. Don't let this simplicity fool you. For how quickly we are back in the traffic in our heads!

Five

Everyday Mindfulness

What follows now are mini-essays on aspects of mindful living. They address the *informal* side of mindfulness practice. Later we will cover *formal* practices like meditation. Together, informal and formal approaches can be seen as the left and right hand tilling our garden of mindfulness. The everyday, informal practice spreads many seeds of mindfulness wide. The formal plants a few seeds deep. Informally, the day is punctuated with mindful moments; formally, we stake a few practices in particular places and times. I suddenly sip my steaming tea with full attention (informal). I sit on my cushion most days at 6 in the morning for 30 minutes (formal). Now we go into the many ways mindfulness can be spread widely in our everyday life.

The Art of (Not) Seeing

Narcissus stared. He stared in that desperate grasping to possess his own image. Some part of us knows what that mythical gesture means. For we, too, are entranced and stare into our self-mirroring thoughts, interior talk, and images. We, too, are unable to take our eyes away. We stare but no longer see. For as we shall see, this seeing does not grasp in order to possess and hold. It receives what is freely given and lets it go. Narcissus dissolves into the pond of pure and simple awareness. A state of openness shrinks the self staring at its own image. Milner's wide focus with the whole body brought her the release the narrow focus in the head did not. The little self – our personal elf – lives in the little house of the head.

Mindfulness practice begins with the paradox of not trying and not expecting. Most of the time, we strive with willed effort to gain some definite end. "Keep your eye on the goal and achieve it!" "Pay tense attention to what you are to learn!" "Try, then try again!" These reflect our conventional wisdom on the path of success. But this very goal focus and effort actually inhibit mindfulness. Odd.

Aldous Huxley in *The Art of Seeing* wrote a fascinating account of how strained vision impairs seeing. Based on the Bates Method, Huxley used these very principles of relaxing vision from the habits of staring and fixation to vastly improve his life-long poor eyesight. The same principles and practices parallel the promotion of mindfulness.

"Dynamic relaxation is that state of body and mind which is associated with normal and natural functioning." "Malfunctioning and strain tend to appear whenever the conscious 'I' interferes...either by trying too hard to do well, or by feeling unduly anxious about possible mistakes" (*The Art of Seeing*). Huxley noted that once strained staring created poorer seeing, the tendency was to stare even more to correct the problem. Straining and willing create tension. Tension prods poor posture and restricted breathing. And on and on in a spiraling vicious cycle. For most people, the idea of willed effort is automatically associated with muscular tightening. The benefits Aldous experienced came gradually from a number of exercises designed to reverse the habits of staring and straining to see. The exercises restored natural relaxation that sharpened his vision. He credited this method with preventing his visual decline toward functional blindness.

Mindfulness requires the same relaxation from willed effort and outcome focus. Like vision, it is a kind of "seeing." Trying to produce an outcome blocks this seeing. Being open and curious invites the mood of mindfulness. Mason and Hargreaves (*British Journal of Medical Psychology, 2001*) looked at who most benefited from a course on mindfulness. Those who held flexible expectations in contrast to those who demanded fixed, rather rigid outcomes experienced the most profound impact from the training.

Rigid expectations are a symptom of black-and-white thinking. This kind of thinking is gripped by the illusion of extremes: Something is either all there or not there. I am either benefiting in a big way or not at all. I am either fully mindful or not mindful at all. So here is a word about benefits and about mindfulness itself.

Some benefits are rather quick and dramatic, but most benefits of the practice are gradual. It is the gradual that is easily missed. As for mindfulness itself, this state of mind presents in degrees, usually. My campus event and Milner's examples are bold and clear. But what about times in which emotions or our interior commentaries are loud, when stress is soaking our system? Mindfulness is still present when there are attempts to feel and observe what is going on. Reaching states of calm and bliss is not the point. Developing degrees of freedom from the undertow of the self-obsessed mind is.

We take up a set of practices to undo our habit of mental staring. So we begin with open expectations. We bring along curiosity, patience, non-judgment of ourselves and of the practice. We approach mindfulness more like play than striving for results. We are sensing with a relaxed wide focus. We are learning to see in the present.

I recommend that you take each of the following sections one at a time. Read, for example, *On Slowing Down* slowly. Take it in. Then put the book down and live with what comes to you out of the section. Let it penetrate. Otherwise, you may unwittingly rush to pack in more and more information and miss the music of the piece you just read.

On Slowing Down

Rush, hurry, and the pressure of too little time are perhaps the biggest blocks to being in mindful time. "I don't have time," is the common complaint I hear most often from sincere people struggling to practice mindfulness.

Breaking from furrowed thought
your eyes pour into
wild and laughing blue:
a patch of summer bluebonnets!

Nearby, a hummingbird
on way to somewhere else
halts midair to nectarize
a tiny honeysuckle horn.

To busy be
or not?
To dilate
or to
dart?

If there was only one practice available to evoke mind-fulness, I would choose *slowing down.*

Our heads are usually traveling so fast, our poor bodies get numbed and dragged from behind. When we slow down, our bodies and senses move into present view. It is as if the speeding mind suddenly notices a change in tempo and opens a space to ask what is going on.

Deliberately slow your walking speed and you feel in this opened space the sensations in your legs and sense your surroundings. Slow and deepen the breath, feeling a shift from mental chatter to sensations of air moving into nostrils, chest, belly. Slow your listening and speech and sense the other's physical presence, the emotional impact of his words, and a clearer sense of thoughts arising in response. Speed reduces space and time to claustrophobic edginess. Quietly slowing down enlarges the space of present happenings.

A day can be started in a rush. Upon awakening, thoughts and commands, dreads or desires crowd the mind like a restless mob. The body is dragged out of bed. There is only thinking about what is coming up in the day. Breakfast, showering, dressing are just a blur. Like Joyce's Duffy we have already moved out of the body and into our story.

Or our day's beginning might find mindful spots of time. Rather than fall mindlessly into the fast lane of our churning mind, we focus slowly on one thing at a time... even when thinking about the day before arising. We slowly walk, take a little time to breathe the new breaths of the day consciously, savor the small pleasures of shower and breakfast. In these moments, we are rebelling. We are refusing to be goaded into stressful speed. And this sets a tone of mindful valuing the present life we are now living. Such a little gesture; such a large return.

A major stress today is the sense of so much to do in so little time. We sense there is too much happening to take in. The pace to keep up is pressured. We are like the rabbit in Alice in Wonderland: always feeling late for a very important date!

All mindfulness practices depend upon slowing down and opening a space to sense and feel what is coming up in our experience. Even when the body is moving fast in a dance or tennis game, the mind is still and observing the action. When athletes experience being "in the zone," they do not describe rush and pressured leaps to the finish line. They speak of being so present and clear that reality seems to slow and open wider spaces to see what is coming and to respond. Everything moves all-of-a-piece.

On Breathing

Mindfulness of breath begins the beguine of the critical role of the body in this practice. Meditation and mindfulness can too easily get snagged in an anti-body campaign. The old notions of navel gazing and out-of-the-body aspirations are opposite of mindful grounding in our concrete sensory and feeling experiences. Becoming embodied, not disembodied, is the aspiration of the practice. So we begin with the bodily experience of breathing.

How can I hope to evoke an appreciation of this golden resource of the ordinary act of breathing? It is present through all mindfulness practices. It is vital to the rekindling of our fundamental state of embodiment, the flashes and flows of aliveness in the body. It is a primary way we learn to directly perceive the difference between non-verbal awareness and the overly dominant verbal mind. It puts you in touch with the presence of tension and contraction from stress. It is quick and easy to follow. Its shallowness or fullness cues the brain to tense before some real or imaginary threat -- or to release into the relaxation of "all-right-ness." It is helpful in more completely digesting our major emotional experiences.

Another Little Greek Tale

She told the story of Theseus and the Labyrinth.
How a simple thread traced lostness back to freedom.
Then she said, You too can go inside your own
labyrinth, get lost, and come out alive.
She said the breath is a golden thread.
It is always tied to the door of your freedom.
I went inside the dark and into the maze of my mind.
I got lost in hallways and mirrors.
I remembered the golden thread.
I breathed my way back home.

Our breath is indeed a golden thread. But we have forgotten its powers.

We are a people of anorexic breathers. We starve ourselves through contracted efforts to be in control. The baby breathes into a bulbous belly. The tight and tense adult gulps air into the upper chest. This chronic lack of oxygen keeps vital energy low. Stiffened muscles and cramped posture narrow the breath channel. Greater stress leads to greater constriction, leading to greater stress. All the while, the golden thread sits balled in our pockets. We only have to find and follow it.

So we begin our mindfulness practice by fully feeling the act of breathing. We learn to sense the difference between full and shallow breathing. We release the imprisoned breath to open and enlarge. We rediscover diaphragmatic breathing.

Jim sits in a chair, supported by relaxed yet
straight spine. He tunes into the direct sensation

of his breathing. The sensitive nostrils signal
breath entering and leaving. Wave after wave
of breath. Only this, nothing more. He lets the
rising and falling rib cage and chest enter his
awareness. He stays with this a while. Thoughts
arise. He knows to just notice and not run off
with them. Notice and return to this golden
breath breathed only in this moment. Now he
puts the palm of his right hand over his navel.
He breathes toward it, seeing if he can make the
hand rise and fall with his breath. He sees
he must allow stomach muscles, usually
chronically tightened, to release. It takes some
practice...sitting...while driving...in
moments before his desk or TV. After a couple of
weeks, he finds he can send the breath into the
diaphragm with ease and sureness. He can sense
deep, full breathing where before he could not.

Once breathing is freed to lengthen, restricted sensations from other places in the body loosen and begin to arise in awareness. The breath finds its natural way deep into the abdomen. The body's center of gravity is lowered. What was once overly top heavy and "heady" is grounded in the body's core. Without this shift in breathing, meditation and practice with the breath may become caught in the zone of the head, losing the body as a whole.

As Jim's breath practice literally deepened, he
found his head reattached to his body. He no
longer felt he was a head ahead of his body

when walking, walking now from his
abdominal center. His breath filled his whole
body. When overcome with thought storms, he
followed the breath's golden thread and dropped
into vital sensations. Like crimson fish
swimming around a golden rock in the center of
a fish bowl, he saw thoughts – when present –
moving around the stable and grounded breath.

Now when stress arises, one feels it in body sensations
and breath alterations. Keeping attention on breathing and
allowing the breath to deepen anchor us while stress winds rock
our boats. The brain picks up the neurological signal to calm.
Shallow, rapid breathing sends emergency flares to the brain,
increasing heart rate to prepare for stress. Restricted breathing is also over-used coping to dampen a distressing feeling
in a gesture of damage control. I try to swallow a sadness or
tighten the chest around a rising fear. Again, the brain reads
this as a threat signal, increasing the stress around the feeling.
Resistance, as we shall see, leads to a vicious circle of reactive
and spiraling anxiety.

Like wasps stirred by a shaken hive Jim grew
dizzy thinking of his boss's sarcastic remark.
Heart pumped in his adrenalin stream. Anger
rose. Then he remembered the golden thread.
Knowing that joining his raging speech inside to
his boss would only fuel the rage, he let the
speech be. He turned to his shallow breath and
let it drop, as he dropped out of his head and
into his baby breathing belly. He saw his

thoughts buzzing and buzzing around, creating
emotional turbulence. But he saw them as just
thoughts, not the script's play he was compelled
to enter. For a while, he breathed free and kept
walking.

So mindfulness of breathing is not only an entrance into
mindfulness practice, it is one of the stars guiding navigation
on our emotional sea.

Where to begin? Find and follow your breath with
full, thick attention. Thick attention is wholly focused;
thin attention is scattered. Befriend the breath, for as you
go along the mindfulness path, your breath will become
an intimate companion. Learn to deepen your breathing to
break the habit of shallow inspiration and expiration. Stay
with the practice until breathing returns to its set point
in the belly. Once you have breathing depth, you will be
ready for various mindfulness practices. Slowing down and
feeling the fullness of your breathing are our first practice
passages.

On Savoring Your Senses

The sensuous world is always local, always present. It
does not live in words, thoughts, fantasies. We were made for
this sensuous world...thinking came much later. Thinking
came as a wonder tool of mapmaking. Unfortunately, we live
as though the map is superior to the symbolized landscape.
The philosopher William James makes the point that the

mind's talent is for ever-evolving pragmatic ideas and theories; it is not made to pin down absolute truth and certain knowledge. We create better maps but we can never merge map with mountains and rivers.

Mindfulness is about renewing access to your sensory world. It turns on the lights of sensitivity to sensations usually dimmed or silenced. We come alive through this nourishing contact. The poet Walt Whitman says about the things directly sensed, "I am mad for it to be in contact with me." Or the poet John Keats in a letter says, "O for a life of Sensations, not Thought!"

By learning to shift from mental activity to open awareness, we remove the obstacle to sensing what is always coming to us in this moment. And what comes to us is the magic of living sounds, colors, smells, textures, and forms. Not fixed and nailed down, but always moving and changing. That is why fixed words cannot hold the fluid world of perception.

Do not underestimate this sensuous world. It has its own intelligence and wisdom. There is the kind of verbal knowing we tend to privilege…and a knowing from the sensed world. This understanding sees patterns, gives rise to intuitions, teaches lessons for life outside of talk and theories.

To mindfully sense, we separate mental labels, judgments, interpretations from pure sensory experiences. Open awareness allows the sensory world in. Focused attention explores specific zones of experience. Perhaps most importantly, intimate touch undoes the usual distance we place between ourselves and the now-perceived world. We attend intimately as though touching the world through each sense. Our relation to what is sensed is no longer selecting and grasping. It is meeting and embracing the sheer intensity of contact. We no longer gather data; we give birth to sensuous experiences.

Seeing

As it was with breathing, we fall into habits of restricted seeing. We use our eyes to split the world into objects. We seek and stare, blotting out what has no personal relevance. Seeing gets swept up in goals and projects. Muscles around the eyes chronically tighten. We look in such a way that keeps the world "out there."

So it is quite a different experience to relax the eyes from searching and to allow vision to soften. Mindful seeing is allowing, exploratory, and intimate. In awareness we let sensations come in. In attention we go out to meet some of them at times. And we touch the flesh – not of an object – but of something pulsing in the world.

For no reason at all, my heart feels a silent
singing. I was gazing out my kitchen window,
thinking of morning tasks: laundry, bills,
exercise, preparing tomorrow's classes. Worry
spun into whirlpools: the stock market,
turbulent national elections. But now -- now I
am *seeing* out my window and am taken by a
sunlit patch of shimmering green, luminous
green grass at the foot of the spreading pecan
tree. The mind, once full of thought, is full of
sight and the heart, too, spreads like the pecan
branches. I look and I feel and that is enough.
I am here and I am alive and I am *in* grass, tree,
light. Energy touching energy.

Begin by letting things come to your eyes. You cannot
know beforehand what you want to see until something in
your sight approaches you. Look around where you are now.
Forget what you thought was important. Give the seeing
impulse and intuition back to the eyes. Explore what it feels
like to really let something fully in to yourself through quiet
seeing. Notice not only visual objects, but feel the space
around and between them.

Why not take a walk in a familiar place? Explore
what you thought you already knew anew. Let breath and
eye work together.

Hearing

The symphony of descending evening begins to play. Night invites the eyes to retreat and the ears to perk. Cicadas and tree frogs fiddle and percuss. Air conditioning hums. Every now and then a voice punctuates the air, then disappears. You hear the sound of your nostril pitch of breath-breeze moving. You disappear into the sounding silence.

To extend the poet Walt Whitman, we listen in to the sound of our own and other's "valve'd voice." Tones shape the felt meaning of spoken sentences. We listen with one ear for words and with another ear for feelings in pitch, modulation, tonal color. Our guts quake when there is a mismatch.

Perhaps we neglect in our focus on information to realize times we are simply content to ride the waves of the other's vocal rhythms and song.

In mindfulness, hearing becomes attuned listening. Just as the visual environment can assault with "too much," surrounding sounds can be a cacophony of noise. How many homes avoid silence by the ever-blaring TV? We become addicted to the "too much" and fear being left alone with the simpler, quieter world. Yet something in us cries out for times of silence, simplicity, and uncluttered space.

Tasting

He wrote a poem-letter to his wife. William Carlos Williams faintly apologized. He found his wife's bowl of plums in the refrigerator. He ate them all. And all he could say was "Forgive me…they were so sweet and so cold" ("This is Just to Say"). No one could doubt that Williams was fully there in that moment of savoring the plums. He lost himself in plums with just a hint of frost and loaded with juice and pulp mashed with tongue and teeth into nectar.

We are a people of speed eaters in the strange predicament of having to eat by shoveling to get even a hint of the taste we crave. Our minds are often elsewhere. Here is a diet remedy: Eat slowly and savor the bites from beginning to end. Then see how much you really need to eat.

Taste the whole cycle of tasting. Flavor changes from the front of mouth to back to the swallowed aftertaste. Go for slow food, not fast. Savor as the poet relished the "so sweet and so cold."

Touching

Touch is the world of texture and density. We use our hands to grapple, grasp, and maneuver things. We use our feet to get from here to elsewhere. Do I ever let myself feel the pot in my hands, the steering wheel, the doorknob? Do I let myself be touched by warm shower waterfalls on eager skin? Do I feel the other's hand in my own, touching and being touched? The full-blown hug?

One of the forms of formal meditation is walking mindfully by slowing down to feel the sensation of foot lifting and landing. Usually we are in a hurry or simply off in our mind somewhere. Streaming through the feet, legs, waist, spine, and shoulder are currents of coordinated messaging of muscle stretch and the dance with gravity.

Begin with something you do everyday. Walking, holding a fork, driving, touching someone. Are you really there? Find out.

Moving

Moving and touch are closely related. Our bodies in motion contact solid ground and ephemeral air. Moving depends upon rhythm and balance. Moving is made up of falling and landing. If the next foot did not come to the rescue of the other foot, there would be only falling.

Falling and finding stability make up the poles of motion life. Feeling interior guides to posture and spinal support bring balance and centeredness. Sitting or standing stiffly or in a slouch produces tense exhaustion and weakness. Moving rigidly reduces natural rhythms that make for effortless walking. Just as we have become anorexic breathers, we have become frozen blocks on two legs. We have learned to inhibit the swing of shoulders and hips. As a result, we lock up the lower back and make the legs do the work of the whole body.

In stepping forth, we risk a fall, if the foot does not catch us. But this risk vitalizes both movement and life. We grow and create through extending ourselves into the unknown and the un-guaranteed. Only habitual and mechanical acts reduce risk at a price: lost aliveness and discovery. Every step is a risk we will find our footing. We trust that the other foot will also fall. We trust we will somehow find our way when we move in a new way or new direction.

Jim wanted to dance. So he took lessons in old time swing. He often tripped over his own feet. Yet the more he tried to play it safe, the more his movements lacked rhythm. What the hell, he said. If I fall, I fall. And he let go to what his body wanted with the music. After a time, even when walking, he felt a different beat in the street. He moved with a new and light looseness. Energy seemed to dance around his whole body. Shoulders swung one way while his hips swung the opposite way. His back stretched in the sways and twists in a most pleasant sensation. He felt like taking more chances all around. He drove a new way to work. He took off his clothes when home alone and danced. He challenged the meaning of a

routine at work and found no one could find a
reason for keeping it. Jim stepped forth and in
risking found a faith in feet.

We now go on with our mindfulness tour into other zones of living. At this point, you might be getting your own sniff of the fragrance of mindfulness. You might be seeing how you must go beyond words to taste its wordless flavors. We are so used to wording our experiences so rapidly that this wordless realm, so primary, is literally forgotten and lost. There is something else. You might also be getting some sense of a part of you being called forth by mindfulness that is you and, in a way, not you. This other you is wider, deeper, simpler, and silent. This other within has a life of its own, if our surface-self can step aside. Who is breathing? Who is this awareness opening wide? Who is the burst of flavor on the tongue? Who is the one moving through you in dance or walk? Is it starting to be possible to distinguish the usual self and this mindful other?

On Finding the Life of Feeling

Our feeling life vitiates when ignored, when disconnected from our awareness and attentive touch. When the subtle currents of feeling vanish, we are left with white-cap thoughts and swells of emotion. Or, we are left with emptiness. We reach for stimulation to fill the emptiness. Feeling pulses with inner sensations feeding our sense of being alive.

Feeling is rooted in our sense of touch. We touch something and a felt quality arises. We feel smoothness, roughness, warmth, and coolness. It is more fundamental than emotion, so full of strong judgments. We extend this experience of touch to our contacts in the world. I feel the atmosphere in a room. I feel another's particular presence. I feel beauty. I sense danger. By tuning in and touching my own direct experience, I come to feel my state of being pulsing in this present.

Feeling is relational. It silently sounds the meaning of our meetings and encounters with things, forces, and people. It ripples through the body, moving or vibrating in different zones in the body. It can travel in the body like a dolphin of grief swimming and leaping from gut to chest to the moistening eyes. We sense the aura of another's feeling. We flash a feeling to another in a look.

Feeling lives outside the mind. We know feelings bodily, not mentally. Thoughts and emotions can be worded, but feeling is a silent underground stream. It is present before and around our ideas and emotions.

Emotion is often charged with the neurological surges of our autonomic nervous system. This system was built to bolster our survival against all sorts of threat. One half of the system activates fight, flight, or freeze reactions. The other half switches back to relief and relaxation when the threat is gone. Emotion surges, swells, and sinks. Impaired and chronically inflamed emotional states fail to quell. When these reactions are stuck "on" they hot wire us for anxiety or benumb and deplete us for depression. Mindfulness of emotions helps us navigate them. We will talk more about this in the section on therapeutic mindfulness.

Yet feeling is not the same as emotion. Our psychological language often leaves the impression that emotion is all there is to our feeling life. As we grow more sensitive through mindfulness, we do come to a clear sense of emotional stirrings in their range from subtle to loud. But more than that, mindfulness puts us back in touch with the felt qualities of the things and beings we meet, the felt meaning of impressions entering us.

Here my use of language walks on thin ice. But here goes.

Feeling seems like a kind of silent music expressing our deepest sense of harmonics within our selves and with the world. It senses and signals being in or out of tune. Its reality is not that of the separate self struggling for survival or success. Its reality is aesthetic. This is not just the special aesthetics of art; it is the aesthetics of living well, integrated, and beautifully. Feeling has less to do with the survival of the fittest and more to do with *care* of our intricate relations to others, our natural world, and to our instinctive sense of some Whole holding all this and more. Feeling lets us know whether we are in or out of tune. In a well-known poem "The World Is Too Much With Us," William Wordsworth captures the essence of feeling and its neglect. He says we have lost our feeling for Nature in our rush for "getting and spending." We have "given our hearts away." And "we are out of tune" and do not know it. Feeling ties us to Nature and to all that pulls for relational living.

Feeling urges us toward integrations. In his book, *Art as Experience,* John Dewey describes feeling as flowing, changing experiences – outside of mental analysis and direction. It is an implicit process needing only our nod and attention as it comes to expression in idea, art, scientific insights. We know of this experience. We know of times we feel what we want to say before the words are found to say it. Feeling lets us know if the expression is in or out of tune by a felt yes or no. We also know that certain experiences need time for them to ripen into meanings and understandings. In our personal lives, we are often out of tune with this subtle urge as well. We interfere with an unfolding feeling by ignoring it or turning it over to our ego's storyline about itself. How many tensions of the day collect into a dark pool in incomplete feelings left to stagnate?

Let's illustrate some points.

1. Feeling out of and in tune:

   Jim's life before his dance lessons was flat. His pursuit of success as a suited middle manager brought security and a few perks of recognition. But little else. The universe was there in abstract, but what did that really mean to him? People were there, a wife and daughter, but routine and the endless stress of lists left home life dry. He signed up for meditation and dance lessons. He began to move and to open his attention. Small jets of aliveness arose. He began to feel again, in ways forgotten since his childhood, courtship, and the birth of his baby girl. Difficult to put in words, he felt a part of things around him. He gazed at those he loved afresh. He danced.

2. The flow of feelings toward new integrations:

   It is in the high art of the short story that I find what lies outside of psychology's

reasoned explanations. Revelations bud and
blossom from a tale of feeling in its implicit
working from dark toward some light,
from surface sights to depths of quiet
knowing.

In William Trevor's short story,
"After Rain", a young woman travels
alone to holiday in an Italian hill
town she used to visit as a child with
her parents. We learn quickly she
thinks this trip will help her recover
from a breakup with her lover. It doesn't.

In an old, simple cathedral she drops in to wait out rain,
she sees a painting. She sees the Annunciation: angel having
spoken and Mary with the look of sudden amazement. And
from underneath the story she has been constructing in her
mind, the feeling breaks to the surface, not with emotional
drama but with the after-rain freshness and clarity of truth.
She had lied to herself about the happy marriage of her parents, her own infidelities, about her desperate and willful
romantic optimism. Feeling finally found words: "Too slick
and glib," she used love affairs to restore her faith in love.
She saw this in quiet amazement and wondered what had
kept her from seeing it before. It was and wasn't her voice
speaking.

When the mind is quiet for a moment, a space opens for
feeling to appear. The young woman had been uneasy about
her surface explanations. The holiday and the break from

her ruminations that the painting stirred opened a space. She felt the bubble moving from underwater to the surface. The bubble burst into simple and liberating words. She no longer had to fight herself. She felt what was out of tune with her relationship to others and herself. She could now let go and go on.

In this zone of mindfulness, we start with a kind of open listening and see how thoughts and emotions get entangled and nudge each other in spirals of intensity and fixity. Once we begin to get clear about our reactive patterns, we are ready for the more subtle sensing and attention to feeling. We note how feeling arises in the body. We allow it space and a waiting attentiveness for it to ripen. Mindfulness opens internal space no longer dominated by the reactive mind. And in that space clear seeing, sharp sensing, and full feeling take on new life.

To begin to open this dimension of feeling more mindfully, consider a simple exercise. Gaze at your current surroundings as a whole. Start with surroundings without the dominating presence of people. Let yourself feel the atmosphere of the room, building, or space outdoors. Do you feel attracted or repelled? Why? Notice subtle responses about harmony or disorder. What are the qualities that you feel? There can be qualities like hardness, softness, warmth, coldness, flow, aliveness, or deadness. What quality, in this list or not, do you sense? Can you stay with this experience to really let it in?

On Mindful Thinking

So far, we have looked at self-absorbed thinking that is unmindful. But is there such a thing as mindful thinking? How do we come to our finest and usually surprising insights and solutions?

For simplicity's sake, let us say that there are three kinds of thinking. They are fanciful, formulaic, and flexible modes of thought.

Much of our usual thinking is fanciful. If we listen to our minds, we find a lot of thinking taken up with imaginary talk to ourselves or others spiced with wishful fantasies. Our thoughts are used to goad or gladden ourselves. And then there is the sheer monkey-mind randomness of one thing calling up another and another and another. The problem in seeing the limits to this thinking is our attachment to our story making and mental mirror gazing. Perhaps we fear that if it stopped, we would – well – just find ourselves empty, uninteresting, and out of the social game.

Formulaic thinking is rule bound. It is logical but not always rational. Ellen Langer writes about this thinking as "mindless." What she means is that it is inflexible, absolute, dependent on old concepts, and over learned. This is the conventional notion of intelligence and knowledge that results in "hardening of the categories." The problem with rules is that they become separated from the concrete contexts that originated them. This is like an upper manager making decisions on statistics with no first-hand feel of the flow from manufacturing to market response. It is rigid like the moral rule "Do not steal" when a mother must choose to lift bread not her own or let a child go hungry. Formulaic thinking is usually based on authority and is not open to being revised.

Flexible or mindful thinking stays open and connected to ongoing experience. Mindful awareness reveals a reality that is never frozen and ever flowing. How can a hard concept hold this reality under all contexts and conditions? Ellen Langer's psychological research demonstrates repeatedly how flexible thinking from mindful observation trumps formulaic thinking. Mindfulness practices bring us back to present perception prior to concepts. And when concepts are used, mindfulness keeps us aware that there they are relative, judged only by their usefulness, not their inherent "rightness." Ellen Langer's *The Power of Mindful Learning* and John Dewey's *Art as Experience* were clarifying companions for me along this path.

It is hard to exaggerate the role of authority in our lives. Some of it is helpful, but much of it interferes with our own flexible thinking. It can doubly interfere by the rule that you must justify what you want to do with your life and by the rule that only some authoritative reason justifies it.

The Talk

In Small Bend, Texas sat a father and a son:
He asked if it was a job I sought.
No, I said, I want to walk on London streets
And look, just look around. Well, he said,

That's no reason to leave home.

It's not a reason really – and I searched for just the word –

It's more a seedling's conversation with the soil…it's

Something understood in me. Well, he said,

That's no reason to leave home.

No, it's no reason, you are right…

It's more a voice no louder than a feeling…

Pointless to anything outside itself.

Yes, he said to me, pointless to anything I see.

And pointless though it was,

I went.

Sequel to The Talk

In Small Bend, Texas sat a father and a son:

He asked what I learned far over there.

It's hard to say, I said.

I learned that London sunsets light the rim of Big Ben gold,

that English cobbled streets click under foot,

that morning fog drowns light much like beliefs I held in

morning years,

that there live ways unlike our own.

But what did you bring back, he asked.

It's hard to say, I said.

When we are absorbed in the trance of fanciful thinking,
no space is left to clearly see beyond its rant and rancor.

That reminds me of a story. A man was out
fishing in his small boat late at night. He had
not had much luck. When he looked up to start
back to the dock, he was startled by another
boat coming dead on toward him. Infuriated, he
waved his arms and cursed the boat. When
nothing altered the other boat's course, he
became even more enraged by the boatman's
folly and stupidity. He hurled insult after insult.
The inevitable happened. The other boat hit his,
thankfully too slow to do damage. With his fist
raised, his face reddened, and fire words
shooting from his mouth, the man suddenly
noticed it. The other boat was – empty. Fury
vanished and only a startled wonderment was left.

In the midst of taking situations personally, we presume insult, disrespect, and cannot see anything else. In truth, the other boats we meet or bump into are empty. It is our fantasy that spins the yarn of "This is personal." Or put another way: How can we be insulted if our own boat is empty, if there is only mindful awareness?

In the open sky of mindful seeing, we are learning to notice all kinds of thinking as just thinking. We see the addictive pull to what Marion Milner called "blind thinking." Whether we choose to go with a thought or not, we are free. We are neither the thought nor the thinker. We are just the beholder of what is coming and going in our heads. Just as we notice dead leaves floating downstream on a river, we are more and more able to see the flow or tumble of thoughts mentally streaming.

On Experiential Flows

When not grounded and embodied in mindfulness, we are like the Joyce character Duffy who seems to live a few inches from his body. He is busy in his head, writing autobiographical notes to himself.

Mindfulness begins in waking up from this note-making by simply and openly observing: What am I feeling? What am I sensing? What is going on around me? What are those insistent thoughts about? Our freedom comes in degrees of finding this attentive space no longer attached to the head's commentary. Later, mindfulness practice pulls Duffy back into his body. He feels his feet, legs, breathing, and the vibrant life in his senses, whether or not thinking is going on.

Once you are able to find mindfulness, letting go and being led into spontaneous closeness with experience challenges old habits of safe distance. I have often noticed a pulling back when I am just entering some stream of experience. I noticed it this morning while reading a compelling essay. I would read for a moment, then withdraw from the reading as if to keep some feeling of independence from it. Why this broken contact? An old, rooted habit of checking up on myself. Once I saw this fruitless defense of distancing, I was able to allow myself to let go into the reading and be carried for a while. Without mindfulness (not the same as self checking, by the way), I would have missed this subtle and quick gesture. And I would have lost a choice.

Are we not living our lives outside the real present in order to get somewhere else like Duffy? As mindfulness lowers the dams of distancing, another kind of life arises. This life flows into vital experiences right before us. But the habit of distancing stubbornly intrudes. Watch for it.

Two Days in One

The radio alarm sounds suddenly.
Before the body is deeply felt,
a map of the day is charted.
At first in islands – then by
the graphing of goal and compass:
Islands of projects press
into a floating continent.

Morning rituals of coffee, jog, and breakfast bowl,
like the sound of fog-horns,
pull your boat through the first of many channels.

And so day one becomes again
familiar traffic of insistent destinations
fueled by intents no longer seen.

And at the end of day one
the channel ends in home harbor
where the boat is docked and tied,
its cargo unloaded by the labor of dreams.

Day two starts before the alarm.
A light vibration dilates the body.
As the other one charts maps,
this one smiles to be alive again.
As the other's boat pulls into the channel,
this one begins to move magnetically
to fresh, sunlit forest pools
not on maps and channel routes.

Out walking, a fairy wind wisps
the skin on face and hair,
like a faint breeze whispers across
a field of light intoxicated,
green winter grass.

Other magnetisms dot day two.
A glance from a stranger in a crowd
sends a gust of life through eyes.
The sudden face of one I know
but shall never see this way again,
the feeling of this fragile flame of breath,
the simply uttered word "soul,"
the light between elm tree leaves,
a prick of pain around a just-remembered loss,
the many sounds musically washing
the heart in laughing waves
deep in the ears' conch shells.

And so we are given
two days,
two days,
two days
in one.

These two days are our dual lives. Which one gets recognized and talked about the most? How do you answer, "How was your day?" or "How is your day going?" How often do we drop the invitation of day two on the street and go on being the white rabbit on the verge of being late? We charge day two with the crime of "not productive." Yet, why is it not possible to bring mindful immersion into all sorts of company, including work?

On Working

How do you relate to *your* world of work? By work, I mean your projects paid or unpaid you structure much of your day around.

There are those who define work as necessary drudgery. This is the work of stress or boredom. This is work done because one has to do it to be paid.

Today, after a recent recession, there is much talk about putting people back to work who are jobless. And there was that recent article on the best paid (petroleum engineering) and the worst paid fields of work (counseling, social work). We talk about work as though its basic purpose is to be like others, doing something for the dignity of pay. Or worse, grading work on a scale of wealth production. Off the scale is work that is not paid (volunteering, personal projects, parenting).

When I was a consultant to organizations, I sometimes asked, "What is the broad purpose of your business? Why do it? How do you judge its success?" Almost to a person, I would hear, "Profit!" And that was supposed to be the end of that.

What do you ask of your work? Good pay, something to do with your time? Status, power, acknowledgement?

Here is my view: Work for pay (status, power) is a lower order but not unimportant reason for working. Our vital living is lowered if that is the main purpose for work. I believe we are deeply drawn to work not for profit but for something larger and aligned with the values of feeling. I believe we work to be of service and to hone a craft. Profit is a byproduct, not the prime product. When these values are eclipsed by others, we pay a psychic price. People working in jobs with little sense of service or craft may demand more pay, power or positional importance to compensate. Whole organizations shift their sights from evaluating and improving the service that gives them value, to those demanding short-term profits.

To the arena of service and craft, we bring the benefits of mindfulness. Service expresses our connection with a Whole. For mindfulness of feeling tunes us to our life in relationships. The Whole is found in humanity, in nature, in the invisible cosmos. We are tuned toward uplifting others, taking care of the world of other living beings, feeling gratitude for our own gift of life.

Craft encompasses a vital challenge, a talent or passion, a way to both artfully create and play. We connect to a craft. We get intrinsic pleasure from learning from it with grace and skill. Craft often is a lifework, for one never reaches a culmination, a perfection. There is a story about a Mongolian horse master in his nineties bemoaning the little time he has left. An astonished student asked him why – since he was clearly a master of masters. The old man said it was because he was just now starting to understand horses.

The attitude of craft versus chore or job can be brought to any piece of work. I can shovel or rake or move a large rock in the spirit of craft.

Mindfulness brings thick and intimate attention to our relation to service and craft. We pay attention not because we have to but because it matters. Service and craft are mindfulness practices. We grow in mindfulness as a Zen student grows her powers of awareness in the arts of flower arranging or archery. Service and craft give instant and truthful feedback. For when we are unmindful, it shows. The flower arrangement becomes a collection, not a unity. The arrow misses the target. We fail to attune to our present impact on another. Our craft devolves to mechanics and a kind of quality and artfulness flee.

Are there service and craft dimensions to what you call work? Can your daily relations to people, to the type of service you do, and to the craft you are honing to do it be a field of mindfulness practice? As you head for work, do you prepare for drudgery or devotion? Do you look primarily for extrinsic rewards (pay, recognition, power, status) or intrinsic satisfaction? Where would you start if you brought a mindfulness practice to work?

On Being With Others

Like the rewards of work, we shape our being with others by the kind of meaning we seek. Seeking to be loved, to be needed, or to be given things like money or status appeals to our Narcissus selves. The rewards are extrinsic. Moving toward meeting others for the exchange of vital energies is intrinsic. Connection and contact, whether enduring or momentary, are our relational life-blood flow. In the realm of the extrinsic, love is a commodity: How do I get the love I want or need? In the intrinsic, it is communion. And as Martin Buber so eloquently reveals in *I and Thou*, we swing between commodity and communion in our daily lives.

Mindfulness of feeling and experiential flows deepens our life with others. Cultivating communion changes the world usually seen through the preoccupied mind. Others are felt in their own realities from the inside out, not the distancing mind's outside in. We feel others rather than simply see and think about them. Awareness enfolds experiential flows of affective energies. What a contrast with the sense of others as self-encased beings seeking survival or self-gratification! Mindful feeling awakens us to our life as relational energy beings.

When we shift from a little separate self inside to the relational energy being, we open a kind of interior window to a shut-in room. Outer and inner are no longer walled borders but border crossings. Wind and sun intermingle with room, air, and shadows. As relational beings we live in and from energy exchanges from other beings, human and otherwise. A person sends a certain tone. A blue tile on the kitchen floor lit by sun-shine sends another. We send and receive felt charges of energies. Some tones uplift our vitality; some lower. There are no neutrals here. When you step into the presence of another, you lift or you depress.

In my therapy role with couples, I witness our separate selves in vicious cycles of suffering. We all are prey to this culturally dominant style. The other is blamed for failing to love or supply what I need. Monologues of claim and demand argue instead of opening to much-needed dialogue. Defensively-armored self meets an opponent, not a partner. The unspoken mission is to win, not to make contact. Communion is hopeless in this war of right and righteousness.

With one couple recently I witnessed the power of mindful presence. We had been working off and on for over a year. Moments of encouraging communication collapsed time and time again into the old argument of who did the other wrong. Resentment, hurt, and fear fueled the need for self-defense. Finally, we agreed to a different, somewhat

risky tack. We would give each person an entire, uninterrupted session to tell their story of pain, concern, and fear. The
story would not work if dominated by anger and blame. So
vulnerability needed to come through, a vulnerability protected
by a guaranteed space in which to be heard. The impact of the
first such session was amazing. The formerly angry partner frozen solid in *his* story melted. There was silence at the end, then:
"I never really understood you felt that way. I did not know
why you did what you did until now."

The gem-like facets of mindfulness shine into the experience of flowing communion. Open awareness creates space
uncluttered with my own agenda and judgments. Into this space
comes *presence*. The sense of being fully here, embodied, and
available unfolds. Thick attention lights up the other's presence
and play of expression. Intimate touch heartens attention with
feeling leading the act of knowing. I am not trying to figure out
the other but to empathically enter the other's world.

How does it feel to be on the receiving end of such presence? It is a quite rare thing in our lives to be given full attention. The usual response is magnetic. I move toward this other's
inviting space and open. Unrushed and not having to meet
her expectations, I may move from my rehearsed and repeated
script to entering the stream of spontaneous feeling and saying.
I have room to hear myself. What I hear coming out of me has
something new, fresh, surprisingly intense about it.

Mindful openness flashes in unspoken moments as
well. When my wife and I talk about our day, the most meaningful spots of time appear in a sudden look upon look. Or
some flash of warmth or friendly energy sent silently, lighting

our interiors. In a silent meditation retreat over a week long, I felt a shift from head to heart when encountering others. I felt as though we were in an invisible field of flowing energies no longer impeded by the mind. We were free to feel our own and each other's presences. It was a kind of floating in some common medium.

Lest this sound a bit too "mystical," I can only say that poetic expression is meant not to hide its simplicity but to separate it from the ordinary mode of over-selfing our experience. We have common words for solid separations but not so common for fluid exchanges. We feel the other in our hearts and bodies, not our categorizing minds. The philosopher Martin Heidegger reminds us: We may operate in prose, but we dwell poetically.

Meeting

You meet me: in your thoughts.

You see me in your waking dreams.

I must become a thought to enter your mind.

But to become a thought of yours

I must lose the flowing feel of me.

I must become a thought in your story.

The place where we could meet is shut.

I feel danger – a pull to shape your thought of me

though I inhabit neither your thought of me or mine.

I seek your eyes to enter there,

but they are closed, gone to the movies playing behind them.

I seek your heart field, but you are in your head, apart.

"Good fences make good neighbors," you Frostily quote.

You meet me: your heart flowing out of your eyes.
You see me with open eyes, touching me with invisible fingers.
We feel the field of energy around us crackling with life.
Our own fields blend and dance.
Our words are polite excuses for being together
below words, outside thoughts.
We breathe in a space as open as a sky or meadow.
Something felt touches, nourishes, enlivens and then
quietly departs.
The fragrance of communion lingers.

Like "Two Days in One," we wordlessly live in a world with others inside the common one.

How do you wish to meet and be met? Does the world of solid separateness feel safer? How many emotional disorders are but symptoms of touch starvations? Are we tragically destined to live as best we can as shut-in selves? Making the best of it and just getting along in life? Or have we been too-long trained in the trance of the distant self seeking survival on extrinsic nourishments? Is mindful presence too difficult or is it now a boat on the edge of a gently moving river, waiting for you to get in?

On Being Alone

Silence and solitude sit opposite the social. They combine as a hothouse for growing deep roots of mindfulness.

Today the postman brought a brochure listing a year-end schedule of silent meditation retreats. Having gone on a couple of week-long ones, I feel the tug to pack and go. It has been a long time since my last one. I do build in time to be quietly alone in my weeks now. But a silent retreat plunges me into the challenge of just being.

Usually, after my first day of silence, sitting-and-walking meditation, and brief breaks to wash and eat, I get depressed. Now I know to not be surprised by it. It is a state of addiction withdrawal. I am torn from my daily structure, devices, projects, entertainments. And most of all, I am stripped of earning my right to be here by productive work. If I neither indulge nor fight the depression, if I simply open to it and breathe in its atmosphere, it lifts by the next day.

Then the next challenge: Being alone with my own popping or ponderous thoughts. What was usually unheard and unnoticed in my busy life grabs the internal microphone and turns up the volume. I am amazed at the cast of critical voices. Here for bliss, I get bashed. Demoralization is tempting: What good is it to just *be* if this is my reward? I just open, touch, and let go – over and over – as waves of thoughts and emotions strike my shore.

After a few days of silence, space begins to open more. This is the space of internal silence. This is the space to see and feel. This is the space to meet other beings: the autumn-reddened maple leaf in my path, the feel of the fellow pilgrim eating next to me in silence. A different dimension, the world within this one, arises out of the mist. Whatever decides to come up in the mind is now okay with me. Just let it come and watch it go.

However we come upon them, silence and solitude confront us with what we have taken to be our selves. And invite us beyond. We become listeners to, not managers of, our world within. We revel in the riches of right here, right now. The heart's balloon inflates skyward like the Wizard of Oz flying Dorothy and Toto home to Kansas. It is not all peaches and cream but it is richly real.

What happens to our lives when we get no meaningful down time? Doesn't life thin to the surface existing of Thoreau's "quiet desperation"? How do we find out what we really feel when always having to pay attention to the endless stream of stimuli? How can the shy sensations of this world approach us in constant noise?

Even before you take on more formal meditation practices, why not give yourself the taste of silence and solitude? Why not silence phones and devices deliberately for a while? What might it be like to take a morning a week or one day a month just to live in unstructured time, feeling again your own squelched rhythm of wants? Do I feel moved to just sit a while, listen and look around, wander? Is there something I keep putting aside that I would like to slowly savor like a book in hand, a chisel on wood, a swim?

Nature and the arts compel us to contemplate. Whether or not we are with others, we stand alone before the ocean or a painting. We are stunned speechless and silent.

Something in us lets go in Nature. It is simply too vast to shrink to human size. We live for a while in its Whole. The mindscape mirrors landscape, seascape, and skyscape. Like Emerson in his essay "Nature," we begin to shed the mental self and open interior windows.

> *Standing on the bare ground – my head*
> *bathed by the blithe air and uplifted*
> *into infinite space – all mean egotism*
> *vanishes. I become a transparent*
> *eyeball; I am nothing; I see all...*

The breath deepens; we come alive. The poet Seamus Heaney depicts in "Postcript" how Nature's untamable power awakens the sense of "You are neither here nor there, /A hurry through which known and strange things pass/As big soft buffetings come at the car sideways/And catch the heart off guard and blow it open." The surface-self is blown away as a larger seeing opens. Why did early monasteries and meditation centers move to desert and forest? Could it be that our concreted, logically laned cities may attack the heart but cannot blow it open? The TV or video game blinking light at night in a darkened room numbs the shut-in but does not awaken. Words and talk having no home in Nature, our senses and feelings rub their eyes and come out of the dream.

The arts, too, create to awaken. Painting, symphony, poem, and dance still our speed and mental sureness. Great architecture surrounds and astounds us like Nature. To the penetrable mind the mystery of art begs to be known through felt meanings. Talk and interpretations may point but must stop at the border of the speechless. Above art hangs the sign, "Only wordless knowing enters here." Education inspires, gives a cultural context, then says, "Notice this and this, don't let your old ways of seeing or hearing blind you." "Look and listen closer." And that is the invitation to be mindful. To receive, not close. To explore, not explain. To touch and touch again in intimate, thick attention.

Are there times in the day when you are tempted to fill a silence with entertainments or distractions? Might you choose at times to stay in the quiet alone? There are small, fleeting moments of solitude in the day when you can stop in your mental tracks to look, feel, and breathe. At other times, might you plan an excursion to explore Nature, arts, or a device-less Saturday morning? Our mindfulness practice is both planned and opportunistic. Each moment and degree of mindfulness matter. Times of solitude take experiences deeper and broader.

ॐ

Four Territories of Mindfulness

Divisions are tricky. So take this bit about the four territories lightly. This being said, four applications of mindfulness continually arise.

The first is finding our way into sheer open awareness with no other purpose than being receptive to this moment's experience. We usually do this through one or all sense channels taking us into the music of the world. Seeing sings, hearing hums, touching connects. Vacations, momentary or lengthened, are wonderful excuses for the pleasures of open awareness. Plans put aside, we are free to look and feel afresh.

The second is finding our way into relational mindfulness, usually with people. We enter to flow of relational energy exchanges and put off having our way. We listen, feel, and, from that base, express spontaneous responses released from rehearsed scripts and needs. Such intimacies are intense and fleeting and renewable.

Third, we enter the flows of doing. We find our way into mindful "zones" not unlike the athlete. The task becomes a dance that is done not just for an end but for the pleasure of the process. Hoeing weeds or leading a meeting, we have a general direction of where we might like to go, not a specific outcome. We enter tasks and projects like getting in a boat, casting off into the river current, and tuning our senses and intuition to feel the right response.

And fourth, we mindfully meet the storms of stress and suffering. We bring navigational skills to life turbulence. We keep alert and aware by stepping back to see our own emotional reactions arising. Formerly we were simply swept away by turbulent inner tides. Now we find there is a way to be "in" stress without being "of" it. We will look much more closely at this aspect of mindfulness in the section on therapeutic mindfulness.

Six

Therapeutic Mindfulness

Across religious and contemplative traditions, people cultivated and refined meditation as a way to end or relieve suffering. Most of these traditions see the root of suffering as
preoccupation with the self – a self separated from its larger
ground, fretting over its survival and success. This self takes
things personally and from the small view of its world, not
the big picture sense of life. We turn now to forms of suffering and the door mindfulness opens beyond. While there is
certainly pain in life – emotional and physical – much of our
suffering is self-imposed.

Therapeutic mindfulness works mindfully with various styles of suffering. Your style is in there somewhere. What does it mean to bring mindfulness principles and practices to anxiety, depression, chronic pain, addictions, and even symptoms of severe, life-limiting psychological disorders? In a society quickly turning to outside treatments, is there something missing? Are we neglecting our own inner resources to meet life stress?

In recent years, researchers and therapists find principles of mindfulness quite effective in many forms of distress. The key is *undoing vicious circle coping*. A toy I remember in childhood, called Chinese Handcuffs, was a simple straw tube just large enough at both ends to inject index fingers from both hands. Once done, you were asked to escape. The usual response was to yank and pull the fingers. But this usual reaction created a vicious circle. The more you pulled, the more the straw tube tightened around the hapless fingers, holding them in. The vicious circle was in effect self-handcuffing. The way out? Move the fingers toward each other, loosening the tube, and slowing easing the fingers free. This is what mindfulness does to help us out of vicious circle tightening and struggling around some distress.

Vicious circles operate beyond our conscious recognition in most types of distress and suffering. Habit hides our intent and our own actions from ourselves. I have a problem. I am pretty clear about that. Yet I not only have a problem but I have an automatic way of reacting to and coping with that problem. I am usually unclear about that, for it is too close to be seen. I think my suffering comes from the problem. Yet most of my distress is generated from my mental, emotional, and behavioral response to the problem. Changing not the problem but the usual response to the problem changes the distress. This is not to say there are no experiences which in themselves stoke suffering. This is just to say that most forms of suffering come from vicious circles. We will explore this interest aspect of our lives in some detail.

Like pulling and tightening the finger tube, we usually meet stress by resisting, fighting, or avoiding. Pain is met with complaint, judgment, protest, mental and muscular tensing. Tragically, the vicious circle in this escapes us. Coping thus, we only increase and perpetuate the pain or distress. The more we struggle the tighter the band of stress. Rather than stop, we keep doing more of the same.

A man frantically looks for a lost key under a bright streetlight. A friend joins to help him and finally asks where the man remembers seeing it last. The man replies, "This morning when I was locking my front door." The friend asks why they are not looking there. The man says, "The light is better here." We are captivated by the light of the familiar regardless of its effectiveness.

Mindfulness practice slows us down to see what we are doing. We observe rather than buy our frantic thoughts. We accept what is happening rather than resist. We begin to see, like fingers in the Chinese Handcuffs, that moving toward the problem opens insights and choices that simply pulling away does not. Awareness and acceptance unfreeze us from old reactions.

In the next section, I will illustrate the principle of vicious circles and mindful approaches to pain and distress. How does one deal with physical pain in ways that either intensify it or moderates its effect on us? We will see the same principles at work along the stages of stress. These stages fall along degrees of stress from acute to chronic. We will also look at a special aspect of suffering, the existential. The existential dimension enlarges suffering beyond its everyday problem level to the level of lost meaning in living. The mindful response comes in at each of these levels to offer a way to open vicious circles.

The Illuminating Instant of Physical Pain

A close look at the experience of physical pain reveals how vicious circles create suffering.

Mindful observation looks at the pain and sees it is far from a simple experience.

First, there is the pain sensation. Seen up close, this sensation is sinuous – full of breaks and bends. Just labeling pain as "pain," tends to make it seem like a block, a maddening sameness. But as a living experience, pain usually moves in throbs, pulsings, stabs. Pain is made up of micro movements we simply do not notice under the sign "pain." Our first mindful challenge in meeting pain is to release descriptions and allow it to be what it is – a vivid sensation that often moves.

Second, there is not only the label of pain but judgments about it. Usually the judgment is that pain is bad, is an enemy. It is to be resisted, escaped, or fought.

Third, judgments feed a host of reactions. I complain, protest, fall into self-pity – at least in my head. I tighten muscles as prolonged winces to pain. I restrict my breathing as stress around the pain increases. I try to push through it or to make adjustments to avoid arousing more of it. If it lasts long enough, I get demoralized and depressed.

The vicious circle? The Chinese Handcuffs? The more I label, judge, resist or try to escape – the more I hurt. Pain itself is sensation but suffering is my story and actions around pain. When there is prolonged pain, suffering is extended to chronic muscular tension and contracted living as one who is defined by pain.

Several years ago I pulled muscles in my lower back. The back waist was locked in pain that would not release, that sent sciatic electric blots down my left leg. After the first day, my sense of its inconvenience morphed into complaint, "Why me?" protest, anger, and eventually a kind of despair that it would never end. I gave up running, restricting my movements to sitting. My physician gave me pain pills. My chiropractor manipulated and tapped. Nothing changed. Like Jack's bean to giant beanstalk, my pain became central and I suffered. Most thoughts were taken up with a problem I could not solve.

Eventually, I was driven into a psychological tight corner. I slowed down my frantic complaint. I remember the day, about two weeks after the pain knocked on my door, when I stepped over despair and began to simply accept that this was my reality. I studied my pain sensations. I found that my body was telling me that I was in some kind of muscular

lock that was now the back's new default
position. I started going for walks. The back
would increase its seize after fifty feet or so. At
first I gave up and went back home. But on my
third day of walk trials, I did not go back. I
stopped, paused, took a deep breath. I pulled
my right knee by hand up and into my waist.
Then the same with my left. Lo and behold,
the seizing briefly loosened. I walked on a bit
more. When the back seized more, I stopped,
paid attention to the sensation, breathed,
and stretched. Gradually I completed the
walk around the block and gradually the back
unlearned its lock.

I learned so much through this encounter with back
pain. It was certainly humbling if not humiliating to see me
wilt under the pain. I saw the difference between allowing the sensation of pain and the suffering created when I
judged and then resisted it. I had created my own suffering
from frantic finger pulls on my straw tube of pain. Yet the
real point of this story is not triumph over pain. Many have
pain conditions that persist and perpetuate with no present
way to undo it. No, the real point is what it meant for me
to move from mindless reacting to pain to a more mindful
meeting with pain. There is a difference between sensation
and suffering.

Let's look at how this way to suffering insinuates itself
into our everyday reactions to stress, chronic stress, and existential suffering.

Coping with Everyday Stress

Stress comes to meet us daily. Our lives are literally framed by speed and schedule. Calendars fill to overflow. Inside, pressures prod us to keep up or surpass but never fall behind. Thoreau tells us that, most of us live "lives of quiet desperation." And this seer wrote in the gathering speed of the later 1800's!

Our minds race toward a future. Things to get done, things to avoid, desires to appease. Or, we are dragging a past of the unfinished, the regretted, the feared or resented.

Our bodies register stress as unnoticed muscles tighten and emotion's flow is dammed. Breath thins and grows shallow. Posture, like a young tree under chronic wind, bends and contorts. Energy eaten by stress exhausts or irritably agitates us. Life feels drawn, physically and psychologically, into smaller and smaller spaces. We begin to live lives too small and tight to move around in freely.

Even our diversions run on speed. News bites with bytes. Advertisements flash into our blinkered brains. Movies tumble scenes of sheer action without quiet spaces to see the subtle richness of character. Savoring a special meal or friendship turns into funneling fast food or speed texting.

We are told that around 75% of visits to physicians are not rooted in the physical but the psychological. Stress breaks through the body like boils. We ache in head, back, and joints from inflammation fired by stress. Our immune systems weaken, leaving us susceptible to virus or bacteria. Blood pressure spikes. The brain strokes as the heart writhes under its congested canals.

Like cooking frogs by slowly turning up the pot's heat until it is frog-late for alarm and escape, we do what others around us do and call it the normal heat of living.

Do I exaggerate? Perhaps. But don't we usually do the opposite and minimize the cost of stressed living?

There is rather weird good news. While outer stressful events are often beyond our control, inner stress reactions are not. It turns out that the majority of our stress comes from the way we cope with it. Remember the example of pain? We can alter the way we cope.

Enter mindful observation. As we step back and see our patterns of reaction, we are surprised and humbled by the vicious circles we create in the face of stress. We find we literally cope with stress in ways that increase and perpetuate it. Let's call it resistance coping to distinguish it from the healthier form of release coping. Mindfulness formal and informal practices reveal the nature of these two ways of meeting stress and their results. Waking up in the midst of stress mindfully, we become free to choose one way or the other.

My Two Alarm Experiences

Even after years of practicing mindfulness, I slip into times of neurotic reacting or resistance coping. Within two weeks, I was given the same stressor and a blessed opportunity to learn from the first in time for the second.

I often come home for lunch. One day I came in too fast and opened the door wide enough to set

off the alarm system motion detector. Suddenly I
was surrounded by what sounded like
ambulance sirens in the kitchen! It was an urban
episode of shock and awe.

I reacted with panic. My heart raced, adrenalin
coursed into my inner emergency response, and
I fed this the fuel of catastrophic thoughts. What
if my neighbors could hear this? What if the
police and fire department have been
called? How the hell do I turn this thing off? And
on and on. With each thought my panic grew.

And I made it even worse. Rapidly entering my
alarm code, I fumbled and missed the numbers.
Then I ran over to the phone in the kitchen to
call the alarm company to tell them what
happened and to get them to tell me what to do.
When I got someone on the phone, I could
not hear them for the holocaust heralding
alarms!

Finally, exhausted yet wired, I managed to go
back to the alarm panel and get in the right code.
Sirens silenced.
I was humiliated. An experienced meditator, I
should have known better. But there you are. I
was reminded I am still a traveler on the path of
mindfulness. I am still neurotic in part.

Two weeks later. I came home for lunch. I
opened the kitchen door too wide. Then– you got
it – sirens from hell blared again!

But this time I caught myself. Feeling my body, I
sensed heart racing, muscles and breath
beginning to contract. I "heard" catastrophic
thoughts arise and yell for me to follow them. I
paused and shifted into observing. I opened my
breathing. Then I slowly went to the alarm panel
and quietly entered the code. Sirens
silenced. The body's emergency reactions –
because I was not feeding them – quieted and
calmed within five minutes.

What a difference!

These two episodes evoked both resistance and release
styles of coping. One was automatic and the other required
mindfulness.

Resistance coping is The Chinese Handcuff principle. I
internally resist, protest, and struggle with the current event
and arising distress. The more I struggle, the greater the distress and ineffective action. My first alarm reaction resulted
in escalating panic and bumbling efforts to escape. Notice
how I fed the very tiger I was trying to escape. Instead of
simple acceptance of the alarm experience, I flew into fear
thoughts and pressure to find an escape. Psychologist Steven
Hayes has written about this as "experiential avoidance" and
provided psychological research evidence to suggest it may be
the underlying principle in most emotional disorders.

Release coping is mindfulness based. I pause in the face
of mounting distress and observe. I accept the situation rather
than argue with it. I shift toward feeling my response, opening

my breath, and slowing down inside. I am aware of stress thoughts and emotions but I do not identify or overly focus on them. I then choose the response I see will be most effective. Psychological research has shown over and over again the superiority of "exposure" as a way to reduce phobias and specific fears. In this approach, the person is invited to enter the feared situation, feel the fear, and then learn to accept it without enacting the old resistance reactions.

Release coping releases the resistance impulse. It opens and objectively assesses the situation. Fear thoughts are noted but released.

The hunters of monkeys in some areas of Africa set up a situation to trap a monkey by enticing it to react with resistance. A hole about the size of an un-fisted monkey hand is cut in a tree. Inside the hole, they place a banana. Then the hunters wait. A monkey arrives, puts its hand through the hole, grasps the banana. But his closed fist is too big to exit the hole. The hunters simply and casually move toward the now panicked monkey. But the monkey does not release the cherished fruit. It screeches until the hunters capture it. Was I so different in the first alarm experience?

Resistance coping and its vicious circles come in many familiar forms. We tend to gravitate toward certain forms over others. Here are a few:

- Worry and obsessing over future mishaps
- Ruminating over past failures
- Over analyzing
- Stirring anger and resentment over injustices

- Impatience and the pressure for results now
- Over sensitivity, taking things too personally
- Perfectionism
- Complaining or blaming
- Presuming helplessness
- Creating lists that never reach an end

Each of these ways of coping results in cycles of increasing internal stress. Yet we do them because somewhere inside we think it will help. The self-righteous high we get from resentment keeps us stuck in anger and distrust. It may devolve into depression over time. Complaining, like resenting, may feel satisfying at first only to leave us lingering in the negativity it generates. Worry pictures dire events that stir more anxiety. And on and on.

Resistance coping is compelling. It runs on autopilot, just beyond our internal vision. It feels natural: Who wouldn't want to avoid, resist, or escape some distressing experience? It offers the illusion of short-term control like blowing up at a Starbuck's server for giving you one mocha short of the right Frappuccino. The rage-burst felt justified and powerful. But was the rumination over the incident worth it? The worry that you went too far? Not to mention the wary or hostile server you encounter next time working a little less hard to satisfy you.

The beauty of mindful responding is freedom from and even within our reactivity. This freedom relieves the pressure we put on ourselves to be in charge, in control. All we have to do is be alert, aware, and open. We turn the lights on in our inner house. We can hear our storyline without buying into it. We can observe – or we can blindly react. We can find the golden thread of the breath outside the voices in our heads.

The voices in our heads. Voices that command, question, criticize. Voices that run around our house shouting, "Look over here! Look at this! That reminds me of that! Remember this?" Surrounded by these voices, we talk back. And we find ourselves in a closed room with no one there but imaginary conversations. There was a man I saw once on a Chicago bus. He talked out loud, absorbed in a debate with – himself. I was tempted to pity him as deranged until I admitted to myself that I too heard voices – quieter perhaps – I talked back to. How much of life is lived in this hall of mirrors? It is possible to walk through this faux-talk awake and bright and free of such cramping conversations!

Smile

It is a summer day on the bay.
This morning amidst a jostle
of coffee and cigarettes
a small group of men gather
to debate and devour the philosophy
of how we can know for sure.

Voices rise and fingers point.
The mind itself is on trial; witnesses are called;
contradictions countered.
A chair, a small white shell, a spot of light –
each questioned and their speechless
testimonies cross-examined.

At mid morning, a sandaled woman
in a sundress saunters
through spasms of speech.
She walks across the raucous room
as though feet could touch the surface
of such storm waters and not sink.

The men stop for a moment
just before she closes the screened back door
and knows again for the first time
the sun warmth on her chest.
Turning back, the men question that slight
mona lisa smile some thought they saw.

These voices sound so authoritative and intelligent! It is
our own runaway train of ceaseless talk and searing analysis.
Yet there is a part of us capable of walking through the room
aware and apart – smiling.

෧෧෯

You can strengthen mindful stress management
in formal and informal ways.

Formal:

Commit some time to sit and investigate a
feeling of stress. Bring attention to your mind
and body as you meditate, tune in and
simply observe. Can you separate the body's
stress sensations from the compulsive thoughts

swarming? Can you identify a central emotion underlying the distress? Are you in resistance mode, tightening around the stress and trying to get on top of it to control it somehow? Take some time with each question until you can see what it points to.

Now shift and see what happens when you let go of resistance efforts and just watch and breathe. Create a larger space of awareness around the stress experience by including other experiences coming to you in the present moment.

Sense sensations in the body, sounds, breathing, the feel of the temperature on your skin. Treat thoughts like any other sensation – pleasant or unpleasant. Rest in acceptance rather than run here and there in the mind.

Informal:

The second way to strengthen mindful management of stress is more informal and in the moments of your daily life. This is a briefer application of the process described above. We will call it catch, release, and breathe. Some stress signal is caught. It may be certain kinds of thoughts, a process like worrying, an emotion like irritation, or a distinct sensation in the body like tightening neck muscles. You will find you are able to catch certain signals before you are aware of others. Once caught, pause and slow

down and step back. Release your narrow
focus on the signal and let your awareness widen
to include other sensations. Bring breathing into
a central place. Expand the space of breathing by
lengthening and deepening it. Let it surround
the stress experience as well. Be aware of
yourself now as this spacious being, aware but
not identified with the stress experience. Rest
there a moment, then go on.

෴

From Acute to Chronic Stress

As if coping with immediate stress was not enough to
consider, resistance coping over time can settle into enduring
conditions. Even more extreme, conditions can become styles
of living.

When stress turns from acute to chronic, when brain
and behavioral reactions dig in deeply, we move from situational distress to conditions of anxiety or depression. The
longer the stress, the more exhausted we become. And the
more exhausted, the less resourceful we are in dealing with
stress. Chronic stress lowers resilience and immune resistance.
Distress becomes bigger and more easily triggered. It would be
like coming home to your alarm sirens going off daily while
you rely more and more on panicked reactions.

Joan joined the US Army when she was 20.
Filled with passion to serve, she hoped for a

career there. She shipped to Afghanistan.
Schooled in the local language, Joan
translated intercepted messages from the
Taliban. Her commanding officer depended
heavily upon her, for lives of other soldiers
were at stake.

At first, Joan was excited and stimulated by the
assignment. She learned to be in a constant state
of red alert. Her ability to focus seemed to
intensify many times over.

Over time, Joan struggled with relaxing enough
to go to sleep. Her excitement mixed with
anxiety over letting others down. She lived on
wired energy. She averted several near disasters
through translating plots and by being on the
constant lookout for any sign of something
amiss: An unidentified car, a distant shout, a
look from a stranger instantly sparked fear.

After a time, Joan was assigned to return to the
States. She was given six months to take courses
at a college and to decide whether or not to sign
up again for war duty.

In the classroom, Joan noticed she was more on
edge than other students. She went at a fast pace.
She reacted impatiently to other's "stupidity and
complacency." And she still found it hard to
sleep.

Joan began to drink heavily "in order to wind
down." She went through two relationships like

lightning as she went from irritability to rage at rapid speed. She began to think she was going crazy.

Ashamed of her symptoms, Joan narrowed her life to school and home. She stopped going on dates or hanging out with friends. She lived on the Internet and movies.

Several months into this way of life, Joan knew she was depressed. She thought of suicide. She quit the Army and took a simple, low pay, low stress job in a library.

Joan's life had changed. She believed there was no way out except to lower her expectations and just get by day to day.

Joan's downward spiral is a dramatic example of what can happen with many chronically stressful lives. She went from the excitement of stressful challenges to an inability to turn off her emergency alert system. As she lost the ability to sleep and relax, she exhausted her inner resources. Perhaps her reactions were appropriate to a war zone. But she brought those same – now conditioned – reactions to an environment no longer demanding attention for survival. Always anxious, losing relationships, fearful of any challenge that might turn up the heat of stress, Joan became demoralized. She adapted her life to her over-reactivity. She now lived only to make it day to day. Without knowing it, Joan was trapped inside vicious circles.

Joan knew she was in trouble. Her shrunken life suffocated her. Puzzling over what to do – medications, psychotherapy, alternative healing approaches – she noticed a sign in the library announcing a mindfulness program. In it, people would be introduced to mindfulness practices and the mindful approach to meeting one's stress. She signed up.

What she learned in the mindfulness class surprised her. While her wartime stressors were quite real, the problem was her conditioned sense of ever present danger. Her body and emotional systems were only doing what they were told: to live on red alert as if her life depended on it. To allow herself to readjust, she needed a different kind of relationship to her wired and anxious state. She saw when she meditated how she tried to control or suppress her distress and tension. And she saw a vicious circle: the more she judged and resisted rather than opened and accepted, the longer and more intense her distress became. It wasn't easy. But Joan was able to use her military discipline and endurance along with newer attitudes of patience and gentleness. For the first time, Joan allowed her feelings to be whatever they were. She learned to work flexibly with her attention. There were times to simply touch and be with her discomfort. There were times to unlock her constant vigilance and shift to places like the breath. At first, resulting relaxation felt

threatening. She understood this as the fear of
letting one's guard down in dangerous
surrounds. She did not judge this fear.
She accepted and understood it – coaxing it to
gradually let go into being in the present
moment.

Six months later, Joan was sleeping through
most of the night. She was going out of the safe
haven of her apartment to have fun with friends.
And she was now thinking about a more
rewarding and challenging career

I wonder what would have happened if Joan's Army company had introduced mindfulness along with survival training.
In essence, she learned only one appropriate response to her
mission: be wired for emergencies. It was just assumed that
people knew when to relax. Mindfulness brings together the
wakeful attention required for key tasks and de-fused awareness. Within this spacious awareness, this gentle watchfulness,
there is allowing and letting go. Joan might have found that she
could balance alertness with self-care. In the space of mindful
openness, Joan could have touched her fear rather than reject-
ing it. Splitting the self into acceptable and unacceptable parts
generates a tension, an inner conflict that only grows. There
was the war outside and the war inside Joan.

How much of your life is shaped to fit your stress? This
is a kind of question that can be silently held in meditation. Ask
and then watch what comes forward from your depths. Is there
a sense of having made life too small? Is there a wind of sadness
or grief over what has claimed your energies – and what has not?

When living with chronic stress hardens into a condition, original ideals and the energies that supported them vanish. We go into a profession, trade, organization, or relationship with helium balloons of high hopes. Perhaps we only saw the sunny rather than the shadow sides of the venture. But the shadow hides and holds the unseen difficulties, obstacles, and sacrifices. Who knew that work, the politics of groups, and the sensitivities in relationships would demand so much of us? Who knew that one might not rest or relax in a war zone? So we say, "Okay, just a little longer to get on top of this!" And a little longer lengthens into a lot longer. Under the continual crush of chronicity, we gradually collapse into unacknowledged despair. We wake up one morning and wonder, "Where have I been? Where am I going?"

It is here that we hear the inner invitation to listen anew to ourselves. Simply, directly, openly – no more rationalizing. We let ourselves feel what we feel. We drop the language of victory and triumph. We see what we can do and what we cannot – without complaint or self-condemning. Mindful space expands to take in the big picture. Gradually, a quiet and private confidence emerges from the shadows. A small trust is budding in our own intuitive compass. Fingers loosen the Chinese Handcuffs by touching each other.

Emotional Vicious Circles

Anxiety, anger, and depression begin as reactions but can morph into states and conditions over time. Observing them in ourselves reveals our participation in them. An emotion arises, a judgment comes forward, a story is inwardly written as self talks with intensity to self. A small breeze spins into a storm. A tempest boils in our teapots. When the self tries to get on top of some emotional problem, entanglement creates Velcro-like stickiness rather than freedom.

Fear of fear escalates the white lightning of anxiety. Fear of fear leads to greater resistance and the desperation to escape. The tail we chase is our own. Helplessness and the dread of everlasting down-ness deepens and darkens the blues into depression. The more the blues weigh heavily on the heart, the more one ruminates on remembrances, and the more depression digs in. Enter self-protection. To live with depression, one backs off from commitments and engagements. Isolation from work and others gives so much more time to dwell in despair thinking. Dwelling in despair darkens the blue ink spilling in larger pools on life's page.

Or take anger and resentment. Often these emotional states are quickly chosen and encouraged over more vulnerable ones, like sadness or like fear. Being red beats being blue or electric white. Red feels strong. One becomes a threat to be respected, not a victim threatened. Power stories surround anger – usually unacknowledged. Resentment has a juicy taste of self-righteousness. This story reads better than feeling at fault. The physiology of the enraged person looks like a track shifted from fear to anger in the split second before a train arrives.

Mindfulness magnifies the subtle stages of moods. We notice inner weather changes. A bit of blue blows in. Memories of last being blue join blue stories we tell ourselves. The label of "depression" settles over our terrain like an overcast sky. Energy is absorbed in resisting the heaviness of the emerging mood. Negative judgments toward self and one's future take over the inner conversation. Bit by bit, the way we react with alarm and resistance to changes in our inner weather determines emotional destiny.

In *Mindfulness-Based Cognitive Therapy for Depression* (second edition), Segal, Williams, and Teasdale's research revealed how mindfulness helps to prevent depression relapse in those who have experienced multiple episodes of depression. Participants learned to observe their inner states with openness and acceptance. In the past, a relapse would begin in small, unnoticed changes like a sad mood triggering memories of being depressed and negative self- talk laced with dire predictions and self recriminations. After mindfulness training, they saw the beginning emotional weather changes and released the tendency to fixate and judge. The released mental and emotional experiences were now free to come and go rather than be seized and built upon. The roots of depression were no longer watered. Mindfulness allowed changes to occur when internal weather patterns were still small.

Being mindful does not mean being always blissful. Being mindful is based on how we relate to our times of blue, reds, whites, and yellows. On some days, energy may be at bottom. Motivation is at low ebb. Do you meet these flowing and changing states with a nod of acknowledgement and acceptance or with complaint and thick stories of protest?

We need patience to accompany ourselves through the difficult. Giving up the rush for resolution, we hold and attend to a process that has its own time. Dealing with transitions calls for patience with uncertainty.

It Takes A While

to separate the horizon of the eyes from the horizon of the feet.

It takes a while
  to release cares and sip your breath like subtle tea.

It takes a while
  to turn from traffic and wander lost with faith in the forest.

It takes a while
  to be convinced it is safe to no longer think of what must be done.

It takes a while
  to let the birds in the tree of your belly and heart sing after the storm.

It takes a while
  to cease making deals in the market place and head for the park.

It takes a while

> *to let the quiet light of your being dawn after gazing*
> *so long at the late-night show of self.*

It takes a while

> *to let the freighted ship sink in dark waters where*
> *phosphorescent creatures wait.*

It takes a while

> *to lay down the little life to walk into the big.*

Staying awake in our moods allows them to be what they are – for the time being. It allows them their own natural movement. But when I identify and fuse with the momentarily downed torch, we freeze and fixate a passing mood into a stable state. "I am off my pedestal, I must be depressed! What do I do now?" And in the blink of an eye, the label and prediction solidify blue into black. Now I marshal memories and fears to prove the prophecy of a downward spiral.

Staying awake needs a softener for starched and harsh judgments waiting in the aisles to rush our fleeting feelings with big reactions. Kindness and compassion toward our experiences counters complaint, shame, and guilt. They fertilize the depths of acceptance toward the difficult.

Kindness and compassion come from knowing suffering as an unavoidable dimension to living. They ooze from the cracks in awakened sensitivity from suffering. In a way, the heart wakes under the burn of broken-ness. What may begin in tolerance softens into tenderness. Touching ourselves with tenderness releases the vicious circle of stiffened toughness. Intimacy undoes the damage of defensive distance. "Tenderness" is a word referring to soreness of an injury as well as the sensitive touch of care. There is the wound that awakens and the heart that heals.

Perhaps there are steps we can take to walk out of the jungle of hardened judgments. Such background judgments hold a mood of suffering like a low pressure system stopping winds from moving trapped air. We admit quietly we are lost. The head that tries to figure its way out is of little use. We see the bankruptcy of our usual ways of coping to control or change things. The impasse reached brings a sense of futility and, strangely, fertility. Change is not possible until we reach a dead end. Then what?

1. Shift from desperate problem-solving to mindful openness.
2. For a while, simply breathe in space around you until you become more spacious.
3. Notice the judgmental ways you address yourself and the problem. Encircle them with kind and tender attention. Hold them in the space of awareness and acceptance.
4. Gradually let go. Let intuitions arising as feelings in the body guide rather than the ego's control center.
5. Be willing to walk – one step at a time – in uncertainty for a while.
6. Stay engaged in your life activities balanced with times of quiet, silent being. You are turning to an inner source of insight and healing beyond your tryings and strugglings.

7. Take note of the difference between old reactive thoughts that just repeat and repeat, and intuitive thoughts and directions that come on their own unbidden.
8. It took a while to get lost. It will take a while to see a clearing.
9. Stay grounded in your formal and informal mindfulness practices.

Quietly grow a trust in your hidden resources.

Ocean's Bottom

Ashamed I am lost
and do not know what to do.

Do not know.

Do not know.

Only letting
lostness lead.

Letting lostness lead
as something deep in lostness
-- a creature blind to ordinary light --
knows the dark at ocean's bottom.

The darkness behind my skin, holding organs and bone,
has a creature walking sideways

unperturbed by my shame and fear.
It needs me to be still, though.
To not agitate the currents
it moves around in.
And, at the right time,
it needs me to
follow
and
not make such a big deal about it.
Just to remember
how easy getting lost is
in the brightly lit world
of spangley things.

We get lost. And we will get lost again. But maybe we will develop a nose for getting lost and disconnected from ourselves. This nose – not the mind – smells the situation sooner. This, too, is part of our mindfulness practice. Joan had to pause a while in her lost and languishing life. She learned to breathe and sit with herself, her agitations, her stuck-ness. As she tenderly touched and held her experiences, small changes in her interior weather shifted. She saw how she had cornered herself in trying to control her fear of fear. She began to relax and let go. As the torque of tension loosened, she had more space to listen to intuitive signals of what she deeply wanted. She started to move away from dreads toward those deep wants. What had become a cramped condition began to break up.

❦

It is curious to me that our psychiatric diagnoses described in official manuals are mainly defined as conditions with symptoms. These conditions are cut out of the vicious circle contexts that produce so many of them, conditions removed from the coping styles that lock them in. Joan's eventual decline into depression and her way out can only be understood in terms of her reactions and relation to her inner states. Diagnostic language and labels are forces in our culture. They are mixed blessings. For some they provide helpful descriptions and hope for treatment. For others, they become part of the way we freeze states into conditions without a healing way of being with those states.

❦

We have been diving deeper and deeper into the waters of stress and suffering. We began on the shore of acute stress and then stepped into the watery currents of chronic stress patterns. Now we will go a little deeper. We will separate surface reacting from deep responding to our life experiences. We will consider recovering our capacity for a deeper responding, a kind of responding that takes us into the last topic of existential life challenges.

☙◆❧

Surface Reacting and Deep Responding

Much of stressful living and its vicious circles comes from whirlpools of surface reacting. What do I mean by "surface"? Surface is what we tell ourselves is going on. Surface is about our personal story, its ups and downs. Surface is life in our heads – thinking about, hearing our own voices talking back and forth. It is emotions driven by this head activity. So things happen and usually we see them in terms of our needs. It is said that when a pickpocket looks at a person coming, all he sees are pockets. Surface reacting jumps to conclusions and judgments. These leaps come from a need to fit events into our beliefs and assumptions. We crave, for security's sake, consistency and are made nervous by the unexplained.

Surface reacting says, "I *know* what you are thinking." "I *know* what is going on here." "I *know* what this means." Then, depending on how you think you are being treated, emotions of happiness, anger, sadness, fear, or hurt arise in an instant. On the surface, human beings are dramas in the making.

Deep responding is below the surface drama. It is how we really feel about something. It is about what something really means to us. When there is so much noise on the surface, the quieter murmurs of meaning go unheard. In fact, we can only hear them when we are mindfully attentive and open. It's a kind of listening in to ourselves. In the section "On Feeling," it was a kind of listening the young woman in "After Rain" finally found. After all the loud surface protests and self-pity, she slipped away from busy streets into a small empty cathedral. She opened quietly and heard herself speak the truth about her romantic failures. And it was not what her surface mind has been telling her.

Surface reacting does its damage on two levels. On one, it runs on vicious-circle coping. On the other, it disconnects us from ourselves, our real responses.

Surface reacting is circular and quickly spirals into stress. Rather than meet a challenging experience with openness and acceptance, surface reacting resists and judges. It is what we called resistance coping a little earlier. Surface reacting is also full of the familiar chorus of voices in our heads rationalizing and justifying our version of events.

Surface reacting disconnects us from ourselves, even though it appears to be about our selves. It turns out that we have two selves. The surface-self is the way we think about our self. The deeper self is our direct, un-thought response to experiences. To get to this deeper, simpler self, we must bypass the surface-self telling us.

In the field of psychotherapy, mindfulness joins somatic and experiential approaches in seeing that when the two selves are at odds and the surface self dominates, a tension results. This tension can grow into physical symptoms like headaches, or psychological symptoms like anxiety or depression. Joan's surface self rationalized her chronic stress, at first, as adaptive for survival. Later she described it as an internal foreign invader she was increasingly helpless to combat. When she finally stilled herself to hear herself in meditation, Joan came to realize two things: (1) She felt her environment as dangerous regardless of actual danger and (2) She was fighting this deep fear in herself rather than accepting its presence and touching it with kinder attention. As she brought mindfulness to bear, she was able to challenge the authority of her fear by seeing clearly what was happening now. Mindful clarity gradually replaced mindless fear. And she stayed more connected to her feelings rather than denying or judging them.

For most of us, deep responding requires mindful awareness to bypass the loud voices of the surface-self. Since mindfulness is so grounded in body awareness, the non-verbal voice of the deep self can be better sensed and only carefully given words of description. People new to mindfulness meditation are often surprised at feeling spontaneous memories, emotional issues, and bodily sensations – all connected to what has been going on in the background and hidden by the insistent surface-self. At this point the meditator is coached to just remain open, non-reactive, and non-judgmental. This means letting meanings arise on their own.

Awareness of deep responding is particularly important during times of stress, confusion, indecision. Listening to this level in ourselves realigns us with both the truth of our real concerns and the big life values we dropped in the rush and uproar of the surface self.

A number of years ago, I held a position in
psychiatric institution. To all outward
appearances, it was a high status, well-paid role
that marked yet another rung on the ladder
of success. After two years in the role,
I felt a growing unease. I dismissed my
discontent as childish and immature. Surface-
self said such feelings were crazy, given the
rewards of the job. The unease grew to become
dis-ease. I was depressed and trying to keep that
news from my surface-self.

One day I simply sat and asked myself what was
going on. I dropped all the talk about why I
should be happy. I listened. The heaviness in my
chest loosened and softened into sadness. I did
not like administration and missed being a
therapist and teacher. I had moved by
the lure of outer success to roles that held no
inspiration for me. I had left my values behind. I
had disconnected from what fed me inwardly.

The deeper responding came as a quiet knowing
with very few words needed to describe it.
Recognizing what I truly felt reunified me. And
out of that reunification, I decided to change my
path in work. The depression, tightness, and
uneasiness slowly lifted. The real work of risk
and change began.

Mindful listening to deep responding is healing. Splits are made seamless. It is always an adventure into the unknown. The surface-self thinks it is in the know. But attunement to deep responding opens to what cannot be known until an inner revelation occurs. Mindful living in the unfolding present is a process of discovery, not formulas.

What questions do you hold in your chest or belly? What has occurred even recently that still stirs in you? Would you be willing to release the surface-self talk and listen a little deeper? Whether in meditation or simply stepping outside the rush to open, a good place to begin is to focus attention below the head. Focus not with furrowed brow but with a space-giving interest – and willingness to wait. Follow physical sensations first. Then let them lead you to a bottom line sense of your felt meaning or concern. Let words come simply and on their own. Remember to breathe in that large inner space of yourself.

Existential Sources of Stress

Deep responding not only aligns us with how we really feel in everyday living, it is a tuning fork to the existential aspects of our lives.

What do we mean by "existential"?

The existential view is what is seen when no longer looking through the lens of the surface-self and its needs. To the surface-self, life's problems are to be conquered; success and security are to be won. We might say the surface-self tries to live as much as possible embedded in a cocoon. The purpose of this cocoon is to create certainty, mastery, and consistency. In the cocoon, we create a self-image we defend and enhance. We adopt rules of living that are to secure outcomes and protection from suffering. Knowledge is what can be coded and nailed down as facts.

Then one day the world of the surface-self is shaken to the core. A partner leaves, a job is suddenly lost, an illness threatens an early death, unexpected violence strikes us. There was the solid world before the earthquake and the cracked, unpredictable world after. The illusions of safety and certainty of the surface-self are shattered. A man or woman wakes up in middle or late age to discover deep remorse over paths not taken, over the poverty of inner meaning in their lives. It is through these cracks in the crust of our surface life that the existential seeps through. The world reveals itself as uncertain, essentially mysterious, and full of risk. Change is more the rule than fixity. Outer rewards and meaning are not the same as inner ones. We alone are responsible for making decisions. There is no such thing as absolute success or absolute failure – there is some failure in success and some success in failure. There is an ocean of unknown surrounding the island of the known. We may come up with workable mental maps to use in life but these maps are not the hard Truth and are always softly in the process of revision.

How do we step into the existential world? With surface-self resistance and protest or mindful acceptance and openness? The way of resistance is the way of desperately trying to put the world of a fallen Humpty Dumpty back together again. It leads to anxiety whenever reminders of the existential cracks come close to us. It leads to despair when one can only mourn the loss of the old while refusing to live in the new. Desperation and despair are refusals to let go. The cracked cocoon is always in need of patching, consuming much attention and energy to try to keep things the same.

Or, we can listen to our deep responding to existential experiences. This means slowly integrating them. Life in the present becomes not just poignant; it becomes pregnant. There is a stirring in the cracked shell no abstract past or future can nurture. Pragmatic maps of life are seen against the backdrop of the unknowable. There is full grieving for the lost world of the surface-self mixed with lost dreams and the regret of wasted time. When I became dispirited in my outwardly success job, I was in an existential depression. For this crisis came when my surface story cracked and crumbled. It was a crisis of lost meaning.

The existential upsets the security needs of the surface-self. It wants your patient attention and willingness to allow existential insights to unfold and ultimately be integrated into your life view. It is quite possible to go through the gates of the existential with greater zest for living and, as the poet Mary Oliver put it in "Wild Geese," with "a place in the family of things." A wider life waits at the edges of the surface-self. There are those who are living with life threatening illness whose existential awakening is expressed in, "I feel more alive than I ever did in my former life before illness."

> Gina was diagnosed with breast cancer in the
> midst of an active life and a demanding but

promising career. Her first reaction to her diagnosis was indignant anger. "This can't be happening to me. Everything is going so well! It is unfair!"

As Gina was forced to take off from her executive role in a fast-growing import business, she began to feel the full weight of "this thing" that was happening "to me." Cancer – and all the internal alarms sounding around it! Anger slipped aside as overwhelm took over. Doctors and nurses talked to her but she barely heard. She rode on others' assurance of the right thing to do, the right treatment to go for – *now*, always right *now*. She was living in a haze.

Gradually, a thought tumor grew: "I could die!"

Following surgery, she was told, "Everything went fine. Now it's wait and see."

Gina went back to work. She tried to go on as before, but something had changed, something was shadowing her. She began to look at her life, a life of all-out career. Few friends. No time for bringing a partner into her life. A little time at the country club and then there was her tennis group, but that was all.

The thing shadowing her was always there. It even seemed to ask her about her life – and was she okay with it. At first she answered a determined, "Yes." Then she wondered, "What

has my life been to me as I sit so close to
death? What is it that I really want?"

She was lonely with her questions, so she joined
a cancer survivors' group. In this group, she
found fellow pilgrims asking the same questions.
With their help and encouragement, Gina
listened to her heart for the first time in a very
long time. Her questions burned her. She was
going through a painful shedding. It was the kind
of suffering like being psychologically skinned
alive. The surface-self was collapsing and she
was falling. She was falling into herself. She
cried and she grieved. Grieved for what? What
she had put her energies into and what she had
not.

From the shedding, a new and tender sensitivity
emerged. At times her falling landed her in a
place she barely knew before, the vibrancy and
realness of this present moment! There were
times between fear and lost-ness that she felt
utterly alive. In the group, there were tears, yes,
but there was joy and laughter as well. How long
had it been since she had really laughed?

Then Gina began to let go of her purposeful,
always-planning mind when she was off work.
She followed her intuition and did what felt right
in the moment. She took walks in her
neighborhood and nearby parks. She started a

small garden. She heard bird-calls, cat-cries,
dog-barks, wind in leaves. She smelled the
changes in seasons. She lingered with friends.
Her suffering had sensitized her all right. It
sensitized her to feeling her life rather than
to a body numbed by unrelenting projects. She
liked this new, raw life and wondered where
it was taking her.

It is way too easy to make suffering an evil. At times, it is
a gateway. Would we ever enter the existential view from our
comfortable cocoons otherwise? Probably not. We are trained
to see suffering as senseless, to be avoided or palliated. We
are not trained to see it as a possible threshold. To participate
in the shedding process of suffering demands mindful care,
courage, and attention. The craving to escape and return to the
cocoon is commanding and compulsive. Various addictions
tempt the wayward and wary pilgrim from her journey home
into the land of entrancing comforts, the drugged lotus-eaters
in Homer's "Odyssey." Not just the addictions of alcohol and
drugs, we can be confined by compulsive work, consuming
romance, people pleasing, and fanatical hatred. As it turns out,
almost anything can be turned into addictive avoidance of the
existential. Even the press to be always purposeful is a ruse to
escape what may come up in us when we are just being!

Anything turned into addiction's cocoon? Anything.
Even certain kinds and uses of meditation! In this poem, I
replace a drug with an inner sound meditation.

Yet Another Little Greek Tale

World-weary Odysseus and his men
on the isle of Libya land.
What had the triumphant fall of Troy wrought?
Home worry, wounding grief,
and piercing wails from blood-stained
war wagons.
O to forget and feel anguish no more!
The friendly islanders lure and lavish them
with luscious lotus blossoms.
Take this melodious melody of chant
and feed it to the heart's attention
and feed on it until repetition's bells
out ring the mind's riots.
And so they did.
Bliss banishing all battles,
there was nothing left but smiles.
Odysseus shouted, "Wake up!"
But trance trumped the call to the sea.
Repetition's bells ringing and ringing
and ringing.

There is nothing wrong with tapping into bliss. But when we strive for the lotus to bypass rough seas, we have turned a treasure into a trap. I once heard a meditator complain that one morning of deadline pressure at work had ruined his peace and calm achieved at a meditation retreat. He had lost his lotus. Mindfulness practice does make for more lotus moments, but that is not the purpose of practice. We practice to meet our every-moment life with openness, acceptance, and the close embrace of what is. We practice for our sea life, not the life of cocoons and islands.

Therapeutic mindfulness deals with not only the difficult in life, it also deals with our default drive set to turn away from the difficult. Through finding our usual way of resistance-coping bankrupt, we take on the way of release. Release of all effort to not feel what we are feeling. Release of surface-self when it glosses with its stories rather than grounds us in listening to our deep responding. Release of grasping and clinging to our cocoons when we are broken open by the existential crack in its shell. In the end, trusting the quiet intimations of a deeper self is more reliable than the fixed rules, reasons, and regulations implanted as conventional wisdom.

Seven

There Is Another Religion, But It Is Inside This One

What happens when we outgrow our mental cocoon? What do we see through its cracks? Empty night or something edgily enlivening? Perhaps it is like waking out of a trance, walking into the brisk night air after being entranced in a movie. Everything appears so new in a palpating present. This is a kind of newness beyond our verbal mind's grasp. For how do you hold a flowing, moving perception or feeling in a fixed frame? Language cannot pin down; it can only evoke.

Everyday language of the surface-self connects us to a culture and has many practical uses. This language works by keeping the world at a distance, objectifying it into a collection of things, including ourselves and others. But once you try to stretch the cloth of this language to ultimate truths, it falters. It was never designed for that.

The neuro-psychiatrist, Iain McGilchrist, in his book *The Master and his Emissary* creates a compelling case for the brain itself holding two visions of the world. The left hemisphere is the world of the surface-self. It sees the world broken up into objects. It focuses on what is useful. It creates mental maps to order and make our lives predictable. It tends to fit experiences into the general and familiar. The world is often seen in terms of problems to solve with mental maps and analysis.

The right brain is the world of deep responding. It sees the world as a whole with its parts like notes in a melody. It sees the world as relational, everything having a relationship with every-thing else around it. It sees the unique situation, not the general-ized idea putting similar situations under one umbrella. It sees the novel, the new, perceiving things with freshness. It feels our relationship to other things and beings rather than thinks of the self and surrounding objects as separated.

McGilchrist believes that the right brain values should dominate and hold the activities of the left. That is because the right brain senses and feels the whole. The left latches onto the parts. The right is able to silently empathize with other living beings. The left sees objects. While the left brain has practical uses, it is dependent on a kind of divide-and-conquer mentality. It loses contact with actual experiences in its rush to control, categorize, and generalize.

Is it likely that our shared Western culture operates and makes its moves far more from the left than the right hemisphere?

Our two brains make sense of mindfulness. Mindfulness views and values the world from the right brain's bias. It, too, is able to see and hold the surface-self without getting lost in that self's thoughts and reactions. Mindfulness opens wide, intimately touching what arrives in this moment with its spaciousness and heart. The imposed distance and separation of the surface-self releases into a relational reality – a field of beings like dewdrops on a sun-sparked spider web.

The world of religion, like the everyday world of the surface-self, is mostly run by the verbal, map-making mind. Creeds, concepts, and rules tend to outweigh direct experience. Ethical prescriptions overshadow the natural morality of cultivated empathy and compassion. Dogma dominates wordless inspiration. Like the left brain's values, the world is often seen as a place to divide-and-conquer in the name of converting others. The quiet revelation is often out-shouted by the convinced, declarative words of generalized belief.

Christianity, Islam, Judaism, Taoism, and Buddhism have all had their contemplative disciplines. These disciplines mined the gold of silence, stillness, and spacious awareness. In their most intense forms, monastic life matured in deserts, mountains, and forests. They fed and balanced the rituals, rules, and verbal creeds just like the right brain does for the left. When the right uses the language of the left, paradoxical insights flash before us. Often they are the paradoxes of mindfulness. The Tao that can be expressed is not the real Tao. He who seeks to save his soul will lose it. Theologian Paul Tillich spoke of the "God beyond God," a verbal shock suggesting the sacred ground of all things beyond the God that is named and described.

Natural religion is found in the nonverbal world. It is natural because it is already a part of us whether or not it is actualized. Mindful contemplation unseats the small surface-self and flings open the doors of holistic feeling. Wonder and gratitude arise for the grace of life given, not life taken by the collar. A profound simplicity exists in fully feeling the present as Reality. We come to experience an intuitive wisdom beyond the calculating mind. Aesthetic feeling, not abstract thought, connects us to awareness of encompassing harmony. Within this Whole one lets go to live more fully. Reason and left brain still operate to navigate our other needs. But they are grounded in the larger sense of life beyond the surface-self. Differing religious forms depend upon this religion beyond religions for their vitality.

Walt Whitman shows us the profoundly simple shift from left to right brain. Notice also the shift from narrow to wide focus, from the strained mental to the relaxed-yet-alert mindful. It hints at the dimension of natural religion.

When I Heard the Learn'd Astronomer

When I heard the learn'd astronomer,
When the proofs, the figures, were arranged in columns before me,
When I was shown the charts and diagrams, to add, divide,
   and measure them,
When I sitting heard the learn'd astronomer where he lectured with
   much applause in the lecture-room,
How soon unaccountable I became tired and sick,
Till rising and gliding out I wander'd off by myself,
In the mystical moist night air, and from time to time,
Look'd up in perfect silence at the stars.

  You may choose or not choose to frame the farther reaches of mindfulness in religious terms. In the end it does not matter. The views and values of mindfulness live in the wordless. When it uses words and metaphors, its language is evocative, not that of hard facts. We all gather there using only our natural powers of attending. The mystic poet Rumi invites us to meet in a meadow beyond all our yes's and no's. There is a strange freedom in releasing the known. This light, this breath, this stirring in the chest, this shining presence of something entering eyes and ears. We come to hear the music of the world within this world silently singing. We are enfolded by the Yes beyond all our yes's and no's.

The most beautiful music of all
is the music of what happens.

Irish Proverb

For the moment, I am putting down my conductor's baton, giving the words a rest. And you, dear reader, a rest as well. A rest in the space and silence of the word-notes lingering in memory, in the feel of your body and world spreading out in your quieting attention. What if you brought mindfulness to this moment? Perhaps you already are. Perhaps you are awake and delighting in your own response to reflections or pregnant stillness. Perhaps you are touching your feelings like fingers to harp strings. You appreciate being here, breathing here, living now.

We now turn to a couple of special
topics.
Pick and choose.
Let your interests guide you from this
point on.

Formal Mindfulness Practices

So far we have considered the spread of mindfulness over different aspects of our lives. Each topic offered a portal into informal practicing from breathing to lighting up our senses, from relational life to solitude. And we ranged from therapeutic mindfulness to relevance for spiritual life. Perhaps we can sense how mindfulness waits for us in each moment we remember to be awake. Now we are to consider more *formal* practices to develop mindfulness. Shifting into mindful moments in our day, we find the informal mode in a variety of naturally occurring experiences whether pleasant or stressful. Informal practicing is like being aware of healthy choices in eating and exercise everyday. Do I eat the doughnut or the banana? Take the elevator or the stairs? Now with the formal mode, we turn to specific ways to repetitively explore and build the muscle of mindfulness. Formal practices are like going to the health spa or gym for more intensive workouts. Each mode of practice strengthens the other. Formal practices are done for brief or long periods of time to deepen training as informal practices broaden it.

We begin by mentioning a much-neglected dimension of mindfulness. It lives along a continuum of sorts. At one end there is complete mindlessness and at the other a kind of pure mindfulness. The degree of mindfulness depends upon the degree of distraction or preoccupation. The extent we are caught up with something beyond this moment or the extent that a desire dominates us, the energy for mindfulness is lessened. There is a place for all kinds of mindful mixes. So we might think about our tuning into mindfulness like an internal hand on an invisible gauge. Turned one way we intensify projects; turned another, presence. Turned one way we tune into the zone, playing bridge or basketball; turned further, pure absorption in a sunset. There can be times of uneven mindfulness in the midst of emotional storms. It is important to recognize the presence of mindfulness whatever degree it shows itself.

> Explore this: Sit for a moment and tune into how your body is feeling right now.

> Now see if your can feel your breathing. Where is it located? Is it felt in nostrils or chest or in the belly?

> Explore what it is like to concentrate just on breathing for a moment.

Notice how in the midst of feeling your
breath, thoughts begin to come in. Focus on
your breath and allow thoughts in and out.

In this exercise, you turned the dial of
mindful attention. Were you able to focus
mainly on breathing sensations, with other
elements like sounds, thoughts, feelings in
the background? If so, you were close to
the pure end of mindfulness. Most of us
experience a mixture, times of drifting and
shifting back and forth from breath to
thoughts, fantasies or other things. And
there are times we find we are mainly
distracted by our monkey minds almost
entirely. All of these are mindfulness meditation.
All of these count as practice. Over time
we become a little more skillful at dialing.
That's all.

The notion of an internal gauge may aid in understanding
the role of willed and spontaneous experiences. We cannot say,
for example, that mindfulness is all about letting go to spontaneous moment-by-moment happening. For we often choose
to be mindful and choose the placement of our attention. On
the other hand, we must know when to let go and simply allow
what is unfolding in our awareness. When I begin to meditate,
I notice the pull of automatic habits as my thoughts and emotions tempt me to lose myself in them. I choose to focus on the
breath and return to the breath when I see myself pulled away

by the power of thoughts. Then there are times this "work" becomes easier, when I can let go and just look at what is happening with interest and curiosity.

All forms of formal practice use shared elements.

All combine three parts of mindfulness: open awareness, thick attention, and intimate contact. I may focus thickly and intimately on the sensation of my left foot's sole while keeping the field of awareness open to other background experiences like the comings and goings of thoughts, feelings, other body parts. Open awareness does not pick and choose, but receives all experiences. Thick attending may select a special focus but does this by keeping background awareness open. Intimate contact is the sense of directly touching experiences, not keeping them at a distance.

All practices embody. They call us from the drama of thoughts or fantasies to our base in the body. They call us to what is directly sensed or felt. When thoughts or emotions arise, we are asked to note them but not hook into them.

All practices depend on the breath. We breathe through our sitting, walking, moving. We take the breath as a companion on the ride of mindful attending most of the time. We watch the breath to tell us our state of relaxation or tension.

All forms of practice trade self-consciousness for curious observation. We are asked to explore, not evaluate.

Formal practices grow best in the fertilized soil of coaching and shared experiences with others. It is relatively easy to describe the steps of practice. It is also quite easy to misjudge the concrete experience of the steps. And it is easy to get discouraged in practices requiring discipline, determination, and deferred gratification. Beginners are babes in these woods reaching for signs of encouragement and caring feedback. In the next section, resources rally around you in the form of workshops, CDs, videos, and such. But like all initiations, coaching in a setting with others best inspires and instructs. Give yourself that gift. I have known a few people who found a practice presented only in books. You may find that fits you or, at least, gets you started. This book offers some inspiration, some clarity around mindful principles and values, some ways to begin informally. It outlines the logic of mindfulness and its paradoxical nature. And it is a source to return to time and time again as you gain experience.

In Umberto Eco's novel, *The Name of the Rose*, an old cleric went to the extreme of killing people who sought to bring laughter into religion. Meditators may murder joy, humor, and playfulness to be grimly good pilgrims. Buddha held up a flower before a group of listeners. He gave no talk other than this. One man smiled. And Buddha instantly recognized him as having gotten it. Perhaps play and light-heartedness are unacknowledged practices. They are antidotes to self-seriousness. You can be heavy with yourself or laugh at your neurosis always showing up in even the best times of meditation. Woe to any of us who tightens so much around the practices as to lose the tickle.

Five formal practices are sensory awakening exercises, body scan, motion exercises, walking, and sitting. There is quite a variety in each of these practices. So we will hit high points. Do keep this in mind: People generally find it easier to begin with the first four first. Sitting is a key practice but it is challenging. Also keep in mind that time in each practice can begin short (like ten minutes) and gradually increase. Give yourself time and room to acclimate.

Sensory Awakening

Jon Kabat-Zinn opens his famous mindfulness class with a taste. He invites participants to take a raisin placed before them. He asks them to roll it between their fingers for its texture, to smell it, to look closely at it, to place it in the mouth as the tongue explores it, and finally to slowly chew it. A fountain of sensations unleash we normally ignore in the chase for the quick chew and swallow. We are simply asked to pay attention. Like William Carlos Williams' poem-letter to his wife, we absorb a rapture of raisin-ness and plum-ness. Beyond liking or disliking, there waits the sheer intensity of smell, texture, sight, and taste. What utter richness.

In the 1950s, Charlotte Selver imported and grew a method she called Sensory Awareness. We borrow much from her. In her workshops, adults played and explored their sensory experiences like children. Surrounding the senses with silence, people would palm an orange and open to fresh sensations of texture and smell, of muscular holding and releasing. Interest and energy arise. How long has it been since we played with ours senses and our experiences? The nonverbal now outshines the verbal. How simple it is and how profound. We hear the poet John Keats in his letters, "O for a life of Sensations, not Thoughts!"

Sensory awakening exercises take time set aside for uninterrupted sensory play. An early researcher in meditation,

Arthur Deikman, instructed subjects to take time to gaze at a vase. As they settled into the experience, boredom broke open into vibrant vision. Blue vase became vibrating blue-ness. An closeness grew between person and vase as meditation object mutated into a living presence. People described it as amazingly intimate.

What would it be like to give yourself slow-down time to focus on some sensory experience? Might you walk barefoot on grass on a mild weather day? Or could you give yourself a bare-foot walk on your floor by feeling the carpet, feeling the tile, or feeling the wood? Might you let your eye settle on a leaf and meander over it for a while? Would you seek out an exhibit of modern art defying any attempt to make it represent something? Why not just enter its wild field of lines and colors? Why try to make something of it? The range of choices is almost infinite. Such exercises enliven. As the saying goes, we lose our minds to come to our senses. The result is mindful grounding. Perception freed from thought.

Body Scan

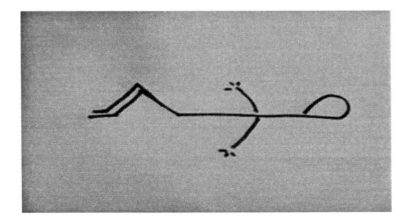

An extension of sensory awakening, Body Scan takes you traveling through your body, lighting up the sensations of areas numbed by neglect. Like a house of rooms, our bodies have many places we keep in the dark until we turn on the light of attention. Becoming embodied and enlivened in formal practice begins with sensory awakening and body scanning. One opens the outside world, the other the inside one. We usually feel our bodies *in extremis*. We register internal sensations when they are too big to ignore. Not sensing the gradual tensing, we wince with a headache, a cramped back, an exhausted body. Yet the body is a lake of waves always rising on the shores of our consciousness. It is a pool of ripples sparkling with sunlight in feet, knees, legs, hips, and trunk. When feeling in the body grows faint, we shrink. Body Scan is a practice of grounding ourselves outside the thinking mind. It is internal sensory awakening.

Made popular by Jon Kabat-Zinn, this way of meditating is easier for most people than sitting meditation. There is more to focus on than the breath; there is the breath as well as the whole range of sensations nested in each area of the body. Some of these are faint; some are quite clear and distinct. Over time, more body areas come online and are felt with greater intensity.

Full body scan takes time, from 45 minutes to an hour. It is usually done lying down. Resting on a firm, comfortable surface, adjust your body to rest and align. Use a small pillow for the head, if needed. If the small of the back is unable to flatten comfortably, you can move feet toward your bottom with knees elevated to flatten the lower back. Let the arms rest along your sides. Take a little time to deepen the breath into the belly and just open to the feeling of this posture. Give up any striving to get somewhere. Just *be* for a while. Practice simply letting go. Follow the waves of sensation wherever you feel them pulsing. Join breath to body awareness. In yoga, this is the Corpse pose. It is a pose for muscular and mental release combined with alert attending. Wash your interior with kindness, gentleness, and appreciation toward your self and your life so vibrant in the right now.

While it may not appear so, this is a skill you are learning. You may drift into sleep at some point. It is a challenge to be in relaxed alertness. Usually when relaxed, drifting off or being in a sleepy haze is okay. Usually when alert, being a bit wired seems desirable. But in mindfulness, a new state blooms as wakeful ease. Be patient with yourself. If you sleep, you probably need it.

Moving attention through the body is mostly pleasant, but not always. You may encounter a part of the body vulnerable to pain. Normally pain is either resisted or an experience we escape in some way. Notice how resistance simply adds another level of pain to pain as muscles around it tighten under our protest. Why not see what happens when you just allow the pain? Take an interest in it. You may be surprised at what happens. You may also encounter a part of the body where fear or hurt arises because this part was involved at one time in a painful emotional experience. Feel free to make your own decision here about whether to stay with it or leave it. If you leave it, simply travel on in the body to the next place or move the body about to break the focus. If you stay with it, again be patient, kind, and gentle toward the feeling of vulnerability aroused. It may be possible to move through it with aware acceptance and learn something from it.

Body Scan, Moving Meditation, and various forms of Sitting Meditation are best learned with coaching at first. Guidance relieves you of remembering what to do. The soothing, inviting, evoking tone of the guide is easily and eagerly internalized. It is as if you are borrowing the attitude of this coach. Later you can step out on your own. Coaching comes in live/broadcasted training sessions or on DVD/CD formats. If you decide to try these practices on your own, that is okay, too. You can separate them, doing parts of them at a time in briefer episodes. For example, Body Scan might begin with breath and pose sprinkled with visits to different parts of the body of your choosing, like a quick tour of a foreign city you plan to get to know more intimately later. Repeated practice moves toward the complete experience.

> Jack stretched out on his mat on the floor. He took a deep breath and let go into the Corpse pose. What a relief to give up his weight to this recline.

> He noticed he wanted to drift off into dreamy fantasy, but caught himself. He resolved to stay awake and feel parts of his body as sharply as possible. He would take his breath into each part.

> Before he began, Jack noticed tightness in his neck and shoulders. He just touched those spots

with his attention and let them be. After a few
moments, he began with a deep breath into his
left foot. He felt lively sensations along the path
from heel to toes. He lingered there, a bit
amazed at how his foot pulsated. He rarely
noticed that before.

He slowly and lingeringly moved to breath and
attention in the top of the left foot, then ankle,
then calf, then top and bottom of the thigh.
Sometimes he felt the insides of these parts,
sometimes the contact with the mat. He came
up the right side in the same slow way. His soles
crackled with sensation, but he had a hard time
feeling the back of each knee. Each area had its
own intensity.

Then he moved into his groin, his hips, the small
of his back, his belly, his chest, the upper back,
length of his shoulders, neck. Then he went
down each arm separately. Shoulder tips, upper
arm, elbow, forearm, wrist, palm, fingers.
Several times, he nodded off. But when he
awoke, Jack traveled on.

Going back to the neck, he breathed into and felt
all parts of his face from chin to forehead. At
last, he landed on the crown of his head. Like an
astronaut, he planted his invisible flag on that
moon. Then he pulled it out and let the breath
move through the tiny hole. He smiled as he let
go for a few moments to this lying pose on
the mat.

For a time, Jack felt all connected, the lights in
his inner home all turned on. He got up and felt
a lightness in his step. He walked for a time
that day without pushing or dragging his now
floating body. He was moving in a world he now
felt around him.

Consider doing Body Scan a couple of times a week for a
while. See what happens and what spreads out from this exercise. Like all practices, it is a gift to yourself.

❧

A Note on Postural Principles

As we move to consider moving and sitting meditation,
it is worthwhile to pause to explore the postural base of mindfulness. This is not the posture of "Sit up straight and pull
your shoulders back and poke your chest out!" That is surface-self posturing. Mindful posture is grounding, like breath
awareness.

So here are some principles to take with you into the next
sections and into your informal daily mindfulness practices.
Our usual posture is either too slack or too rigid. We tend to
center in the head as our center of gravity. Centering in the
head or chest makes us easy to physically and psychologically
topple. So try this for starters: Standing, bring your breathing
to the upper chest and focus on your head/chest region. Have
someone push on your chest. What happens? Probably your

wobble or topple. Now bring breathing into your belly and focus on an area just below your navel. After the push, what happens? You most likely feel more grounded, less likely to topple and wobble. As you practice moving, standing, sitting practices begin with bringing breath to belly and focus to the region below the belly button. Feel that out and use it as a reference for grounding. When you sit in your chair during the day, find out what happens to your energy and alertness states when you sit with spine support and belly grounding. You will discover how posture affects attitude and how attitude affects posture. Change one and you usually change the other.

❧

Moving Meditation

Can we bring mindfulness to the body in motion as well as the still body? We can if we slow down enough. Our usual movements are automatic, quick, and goal goaded. Many of us walk with our heads jutted forward pulling the rest of the body behind. We may admire the grace of the easy, loose limbed walker but wonder if she is going to get anywhere at that pace. Moving Meditation re-embodies the rhythm of walk, turns, sitting down and getting up.

Moving Meditation comes in several forms: walking, yoga, qi gong, and tai chi. Mindful jogging, running, martial arts, and sports can be used as well. A number of these forms risk injury without some training. So I rely on walking, limited yoga, and combined moves from qi gong and tai chi for safe and satisfying starters. They also engage the surrounding environment so little that most all awareness and attention can go to the inside feel of these practices.

Moving Meditation practices ride on the principles of finding, shifting, centering, and letting go described earlier. Tuning in, you find out what is happening in your mind and body now as you begin. This is an opportunity to practice acceptance, for we often find our current state a bit tired or wired with the mind gnawing on its current bone. Rather than judge or resist, you take that deep thread of golden breath, release attachment to the bone, and shift toward open awareness of body and mind as they happen. Then there is a period of centering into the ground of mindfulness and letting go to its rhythms and flows. Who's in control? Who knows?

All movements are slow. Meditative walking winds down to such slow motion you wonder if you can really walk this way. Each step sends sensations of foot meeting earth and rolling with ankle, calf, and thigh. The other foot lifts and moves toward its fall. Breath is full all the way down to the feet. Let yourself get used to the awkwardness and be wary of judgments that surface. It takes a while to get the hang of it. After a time, feel from the inside the walk as it moves through the rotating hips and slight swing of shoulders and arms. Hands hang by your side or are cupped in front of you. Let the spine straighten and align, taking each footfall in supple rebound. Knees are unlocked so that they can shock absorb or lift the legs. Eyes are not particularly engaged except for bare navigation. There are so many sensations to savor. And there are so many chances to see the talking head to commenting and critiquing. When lost in thought, you get a quick warning as you wobble. Then waking up you walk on. From fifteen to thirty minutes, there is just this attentive walking.

Here is an added benefit. Slowing your walk opens an opportunity to see how your way of walking, like your way of breathing, has become tight, locked, and restricted over time. You will find out things about your balance. You will see how your upper torso froze over time leaving you walking as though the legs are carrying an immobile statue of marble above. Shoulders and hips lock rather than rotate in counter point. At some place in your practice, find out what it is like to begin to swing your hips as you walk, to swing your shoulders and arms opposite of your hips. The torso now moves around the spine, the lower back massaged by movement.

Then as you walk during the day, something in you tugs to notice your usual numbing speed and to slow down. You may be walking to your car, to your office building, to your home's front door. Something says, Remember the feel of that meditative walk? Come home to the present, to your body. Live a moment in the swing of this ordinary walk. This is the way informal mind-fulness is fed by the formal.

Yoga, Qi Gong, and Tai Chi

These three practices are hard to learn in a book unless you have had some initiating instruction and guidance. Fortunately, classes and workshops abound. Outside urban areas, you might seek out DVD or Internet resources. I will list one in the appendix.

Until you find instruction, there are ways to play with the moves of yoga, qi gong, and tai chi.

> Jack decided he would start someplace. He could not start tai chi classes for a while. Yoga videos left him dispirited as instructors sculpted perfect stretches.

> Jack started by standing. He would do a few moments of standing meditation. And so he planted his feet shoulder-length apart. He unlocked his knees. This allowed him to slightly curve his pelvic region forward, flattening the small of his back. He released his shoulders that he noticed had pulled up during the day. He felt his spine straightening, aligning head, trunk, hips, and legs. He breathed deeply into his abdomen. Top-heavy before, he now felt his center of gravity near his navel. Jack felt strong, lithe, and light.

A quiet energy coursed through his body. And
for a while, Jack just stood and let the sensation
of standing float in and out of his awareness.

Everything begins and ends in stillness. Sounds break silence
only to return to it. Motion blooms out of standing and returns to
standing.

Jack moved into a kind of dance. He moved
slowly as though his body was moving in and
through a fluid. Every movement was in rhythm
with in-and-out breathing.

While standing, he slowly swung his right arm in
a large circle in front of him. He felt the
awakening of shoulder muscles in the stretching
arc. He swung his left arm. He sensed the
flowing movement from the inside, unconcerned
about how he looked. He then took the arcing
swing of each arm to his side by turning at his
waist.

He next brought his arms with wrists and
elbows slightly bent up to his chest. Palms of his
hands faced forward as he pressed the air gently
down as hands returned to sides. He did this
several times, enjoying the flowing grace.

He next put hands on knees and rotated
them while he stood, first clock-wise, then
counter. He later brought the hips into play,
swinging them in circles like the old hoola

hoop plastic ring he learned to swing around
his waist when he was a kid. Clock-wise and
counter.

Finally, Jack broke into free style motion. He
stepped, turned, twisted, bent over, reached
high, as he moved his body in ways unmoved
during the day. Then Jack silenced all movement
into his centered standing.

Begin your moving practice with walking, standing, and
free-style dance done in the spirit of Eastern meditative movement. Then you might pick by convenience or interest one of
the forms of yoga, qi gong or tai chi.

The body we have ignored is waking up. An aliveness
returns. For a while, we are beings of feeling, energies, and
sensation, no longer the little Wizard of Oz behind the cur-
tains, booming commanding thoughts. We are free to open
our awareness, to place our attention, to intimately contact
immediate experience.

Sitting Meditation

When we think of formal meditation the image of cross-legged sitting comes easily. It either invites or intimidates us. How can I get my Western body to sit that way for very long? I am afraid my mind is way too unruly to be silenced.

Let's see if we can make this important practice a little friendlier.

First, you can sit (or even lie down) anyway you like as long as you as you are physically aligned. Second, do not try to silence your mind.

Mindfulness is not about picking or reacting to the contents of your mind. It is about opening awareness and relating to the content of your present experiences with acceptance and interest. That's it. It is about how you relate to your mind, emotions, sensations, not about what kind of experience you are having and whether you like it or not.

The skill is to access mindfulness when you want, letting the mind take care of itself. Relaxation and mental quieting are usually the byproducts of this skill.

Why is mindfulness such a challenge? The answer, I believe, is that we live much of our lives in light trances. We have come to accept these trances as harmless, even quite normal. Dictionaries use words for trance like being in a daze, unaware of one's environment, semiconscious. In trances we lose touch with any experience other than the trance focus.

We fuse with the subject of the trance. Captivated by a TV show or movie, I am in it and lose myself in its dream. In a conversation, I barely hear your words before I am off into my own associations, reactions, and opinions. I am so focused on a work project, my environment fades and I did not notice the sun going down outside my window. Driving somewhere, I go on automatic, leave the focus on driving, and dive into fantasies of my weekend plans. I make a mistake in my checkbook and I fly off into furious lectures oozing with blame, proclaiming myself an idiot, and swimming in a sea of anxiety. Someone asks, "Where are you, dear?" And for a moment, I wake up. "Oh, I forgot. I am here."

There is a now-famous video displaying part of a basketball game. You are asked to count the number of times the basketball is passed. At the end, you are asked to watch the video again. Shocked, you notice what you missed before. A man in a gorilla suit walks across the court waving his hands. In the trance of narrow focus and mental counting, the gorilla man disappeared! For a full description of this over-focus blindness, see *The Invisible Gorilla* by Chabris and Simons.

A basic power of us humans is the ability to focus our attention. When we focus on something, we find arising together that something and cues about how to react to that something. We live along a continuum in our attentional life. At one end is life on autopilot. We move on habit with minimum attention to what we are doing. This is Passive Attention that blindly follows directions from habitual thoughts or from the outside. We are in that light trance of uncritically moving in a stream of judgments or instructions. Narrow Attention is like the focus on basketball passes. It is willed and purposeful. It is useful. But it is selective and excluding, missing nearby gorillas.

Mindful Attention is embedded in Mindful Awareness. Imagine a large circle with a dot somewhere inside it. The circle of impersonal awareness is simply registering what is happening. The dot is the zone of focused attention. There is the watching of the basketball passes done more loosely within the spacious awareness alert to our inner and outer gorillas walking through. Sometimes we are that circle only; sometimes, circle and dot.

The difference between muddle and mindfulness is not the thinking process or our emotional life. It is a particular kind of thinking and emoting that easily becomes our default position, a whirlpool where we are habitually and automatically drawn in.

Remember Narcissus? Once you begin to observe your inner goings on, be prepared for a humbling shock. Most of our conscious life is taken up thinking about and emoting about my *me*! This feels so normal and natural it is difficult to see its flaws. Why wouldn't I think about myself? But observation lifts the curtain on this inner Wizard of Oz to reveal its costs. Where does all this self-preoccupation get me? What good comes from my fantasies, judgments, reactions, checking, rehearsing, obsessing, ruminating, mirror gazing? You will decide as you enter your practice and see the states of mind and body they produce.

Mindfulness releases the blind hold of Narcissus. It steps back from the drama of self to see it clearly. It separates the waking dream of "It's all about me" from other sensations, feelings, thoughts, and intuitive visions. Once you can see these separate experiences, you can choose where to place your precious power of attention.

We start with strengthening the muscle of inner observation.

Sitting Meditation is an intensive lab for sharpening this kind of seeing. When the strong winds of personal thinking, fantasizing, and emoting blow, we first need a lamppost to hold onto. Otherwise we are easily swept away. To observe, we need the power of standing back.

Enter the golden thread of the breath. By learning to focus on and return to the experience of breathing, we develop a growing space to see. We have fleeting moments of noticing thoughts as thoughts, including voices in our heads, before falling headlong into them. Over time the space of this seeing enlarges. The addictive pull of personal thinking lessens.

But this does take time, persistence, patience, and a kind of faith in the process. Self-criticism is tempting: "I just can't do this. I can't control these pesky flashes exploding mental fragments!" We must be nimble here. Recall that you are not to control your thoughts but to accept them while observing them. Focusing on the breath gives us a clear, neutral experience to see and feel. When the mind acts up and pulls us, we practice perceiving rather than joining in its fray. Then we return with simplicity and patience to breathing, over and over again. You are lifting the barbell of mindful attention rather than slouched on your inner sofa absorbed in the flickering TV show.

So let's get to know what's on your mind. Let's see if you can find your way out of the mind's dense forest and into an open meadow where all is in sight.

გოი

If not sitting cross-legged on the floor or lying down, find your seat in a firm, supportive chair. Avoid cushy places to sit. Your thighs ought to be parallel or somewhat lower to the seat. Sit straight, letting your spine support you. Drop what tension you can. Sit away from the back of the chair allowing only the small of the back to touch it, if at all. Feet are flat on the floor. Hands are cupped in your lap or resting on your legs. Chin is pulled slightly in and down. Pelvis and hips are released to tuck a bit forward allowing the small of the back to unfurl.

Be relaxed yet alert. Be curious and have the mind of an explorer. Rest for a moment as you feel the stability, alignment, and grounded sense of this posture. This is like being a mountain planted on the earth keeping its place through all types of weather. Take a little time to come into your body.

Now sweep through your body from toes to head like a Body Scan but faster. Then find your breath. It is your ship's ballast against the pull of wind and wave. Find and thoroughly feel the entrance of breath through the sensitive nostrils. Linger awhile. Then let the breath fall into the chest as it lifts, expanding the ribs on intake, then collapsing on breath release. Linger awhile. Then let the waters of the breath drop like a waterfall into the pool of the belly. Notice how it balloons and deflates in rhythm with chest. Linger. At this point, it's up to you to select a part of the breath's path or the whole breath cycle of nostrils, chest, belly. Notice how the breath pauses at the point of full intake and at the point of full outtake.

Remember open awareness. When focusing on the breath as a primary target, stay alert to what arises around it as well. Sense the sounds, body pulses, feelings, and thoughts. When the mind turns on its magnetic attraction, see if you can simply notice its activities as events like any other. When you find yourself entranced by the mind, wake up when you can and notice what happened and go, as always, back to the breath. Accept all and everything. That's it.

Well, it is almost it. Combine discipline with play, earnestness with exploration. If my guidelines become a harness, drop reins and saddle from your inner horse and let it go free. If you are unable to drop out of a thought or emotion or fantasy, go into it. Just know you are going into it and try to keep the spirit of being awake to what you are doing. Feel free to experiment. Bring a friendliness to yourself. And learn.

A Sitting

I am easing onto the meditation cushion in my
study, always struck by its firm support. The
pewter light is coming through the window in
front of me. It has recently rained, leaving
diffuse light on the floor. I breathe a couple of
deep breaths, letting them fill my body like an air
balloon. My spine straightens a little in response.
I close my eyes. I stop nudging ideas around
what I have been reading and my list to get
done today. I just listen and feel. My thoughts
wag their tails like small dogs I was petting; they
want my attention again. I start to pet, then don't.

Breath is gently sucked in nostril tunnels and
pressed out again. There is pleasure in such a
small sensation. I follow the falling wind into
chest. I feel it swell, fanning ribs apart and back.
Now I feel the belly loosen and swell. All phases
of breathing are like a living bellows lifting
organs and muscles like an incoming, outgoing
tide. I take in the full range of the breath cycle.
Then I settle for a light focus on the breeze
blowing through nostrils.

A sound starts left and leaves right. I imagine
a car outside hitting a pool of water. Strange how
quickly I identify the sound rather than just leave
it alone. I hear another swoosh. This time I hear
it as a *swoosh* sound all the way through.

Then stomach muscles tighten and heartbeat
picks up. I remember a call I promised to make

but forgot. I join in a flurry of worry thoughts. Feel badly about letting someone down. What if…? What if…? I feel my own finger wagging at me. This all happens in less than a few seconds. I reach for my breath, find it, and let thoughts and anxiety be, with me no longer feeding them. Gradually, there is only breathing now. Another *swoosh* from left to right sounds suddenly.

For a while, bird chirps call and answer each other. Black light is around the eyes. Breathing's expansion and contraction moves the whole body. Another *swoosh*. A thought of a car. A thought of me meditating. I wonder how I am doing at it. Such thoughts come and go, they flash invitations to join and then go. They come and they go. There's a sense of winding down that turns into a thought. A pause. One last breath is fully breathed and now the body slowly rises off the cushion.

❧

In the rhythm of clear and muddy seeing, we are learning to simply observe. We are enlarging the spaciousness of our lives often caught in the claustrophobia of self-consciousness. We are learning to let ourselves be. We are letting the present becomes a home.

Like a good exercise program, it helps to have a regular mindfulness practices not dependent on your mood or time pressure. It also helps to have a special place you create for your meditation. Time invested is up to you. Consider starting small, say ten minutes. And gradually increase to thirty or forty five minutes. Yet feel free to vary the time. Even five minutes is enough to pan for gold.

When you are facing emotional pain, it helps to season the soup of meditation with compassion. Instead of trying to keep your focus purely on the breath, consider allowing the pain to move forward. Simply let it be there without trying to fix it or falling into self-judgment. This is best done after you have practiced earlier forms of practice first. Touch your pain with kindness and gentleness. Get to know the bodily sensations rather than over focus on thoughts or emotion labels for it. Bring the energy of the heart region to bear on the experience. Hold the difficult with inner arms of caring, not criticizing or complaining. Feel free to move to the breath or other sensations that are outside the region of suffering. Explore the movement back and forth. Holding emotional pain in its body sensations lets you develop stronger muscles of acceptance. Breathe and be, breathe and be. You are the only one to determine your focus. Explore and discover how best to care for yourself when you most need it.

When I go on my morning run, sometimes an ache or pain appears. I have learned the hard way to mindfully track this new sensation. At times it seems best to gently run through it, relaxing around it. At other times, the wiser course is to shorten the run and allow the pain to go on without me. With emotional pain, sometimes it works well to keep meditating and simply hold it compassionately. At other times, the wiser course is to shorten the meditation if the pain threatens to become overwhelming. There is a right rhythm waiting for you to discover.

Difficult edges in our lives invite a flexible play of approach and backing off, approach and backing off. In this moment, do I run through it or shorten the run? Listen with care to your own experience.

See your formal and informal styles of mindfulness as partners. Formal goes deep; informal goes wide. They power the momentum of each other. They join arms in a circle dance.

Selected Mindful Reads
And Resources

If mindfulness books were bricks, we would have enough to build a pyramid. That being said, may I offer you some thoughts on some resources for reading, online searching, and viewing?

Best Overall Introduction

Jon Kabat-Zinn produced two classic texts on mindfulness as part of his pioneering program, Mindfulness Based Stress Reduction. The first centers on different aspects of mindfulness while the second describes mindfulness practices and stress management.

Kabat-Zinn, Jon. *Wherever You Go There You Are.*

Kabat-Zinn, Jon. *Full Catastrophe Living.*

Forerunners of Today's Mindfulness

A number of writers paved the way for the bloom of mindfulness before it was called mindfulness. Here are a few of my favorites.

Thoreau, Henry David. *Walden.*

Emerson, Ralph Waldo. "Nature" (and other essays).

Huxley, Aldous. *Tomorrow and Tomorrow and Tomorrow.*

Milner, Marion. *A Life of One's Own.*

Watts, Alan. *The Wisdom of Insecurity.*

Brooks, Charles. *Sensory Awareness* (based on Charlotte Selver).

The Special Case of Carl Rogers

Carl Rogers, the American psychologist, helped to birth the humanistic movement in psychology as a counter-weight to psychoanalytic, cognitive and behavioral theories. When reading him today, it is clear he was writing from the perspective and values of mindfulness before it was coined as a term.

Rogers, Carl. *On Becoming a Person.*

Buddhism

Though mindfulness has roots in many contemplative and religious traditions, we have, I believe, most benefitted from the deep springs of Buddhism over the centuries. Unique among religions, Buddha presented himself, not as a god but as a man – an awake man. He and his followers have given us a profound psychology and a set of practices designed to liberate us from our own self-created suffering. As a psychologist, I stand before Buddha's insights with nothing short of amazement. Mindfulness, as we are beginning to understand it, was a centerpiece of his vision of being fully human. Below are some works I find user-friendly from that tradition.

Howley, Adrienne. *The Naked Buddha* (brief, good overview).

Hanh, Thich Nhat. *The Miracle of Mindfulness* (a small classic).

Goldstein, Joseph & Kornfield, Jack. *Seeking The Heart of Wisdom.*

Suzuki, Shunryu. *Zen Mind, Beginner's Mind.*

Chodron, Pema. *How to Meditate.*

Trungpa, Chogyam. *The Myth of Freedom.*

O'Hara, Pat Enkyo. *Most Intimate: A Zen Approach To Life's Challenges.*

Ricard, Matthieu. *Happiness*

Therapeutic Mindfulness in Psychology

These following works are written with lay persons in mind. They deal with different aspects of psychological distress using mindfulness.

Santorelli, Saki. *Heal Thyself.*

Williams, Mark et al. *The Mindful Way Through Depression.* (includes a CD of formal practices)

Orsillo, Susan & Roemer, Lizabeth. *The Mindful Way Through Anxiety.*

Neff, Kristin. *Self-Compassion.*

Hayes, Steven et al. *Acceptance and Commitment Therapy.*

Brach, Tara. *True Refuge*

Cornell, Ann Weiser. *The Radical Acceptance of Everything: Living a Focusing Life*

Best Integration of Psychology, Buddhism, and Mindfulness

Welwood, John. *Toward a Psychology of Awakening.*

Qi Gong DVD

Peng, Robert. *Qi Gong Ecstasy.*

Best Mindfulness book for business people

Marturano, Janice. *Finding the Space to Lead.*

Research on Mindfulness

See www.mindfulexperience.org/newsletter.php

See www.mindfulnet.org

Mindfulness and the Brain

Siegel, Daniel. *The Mindful Brain*

McGilchrist, Iain. *The Master and his Emissary*

Blogs and Audios on Mindfulness

See www.dharmaseed.org (for Buddhist talks on mindfulness)

See my www.martinlumpkin.com

See YouTube sites on mindfulness, including Jon Kabat-Zinn

Sponsors of Meditation Retreats

The Insight Meditation Society

Spirit Rock Center

Mindfulness Training Programs

Mindfulness Based Stress Reduction

Mindfulness Based Cognitive Therapy

Poets Connected with Mindfulness

Mary Oliver

David Whyte

Stephen Levine

Rumi (trans. Coleman Barks)

William Stafford

Walt Whitman

Daniel Skach-Mills

Authors Speaking from Life-Infused Mindfulness

Eckart Tolle

Byron Katie

Mindfulness at the Movies

How about mindfulness at the movies? American Beauty paints successful yet lost characters along side a young man quietly mindful of the beauty of the world. The Thin Red Line puts you in the heads of men in the midst of war. One character stays mindfully open to the end. Ground Hog Day, while quite funny on the surface, is really a fable of the shift from Narcissus to a mindful-self. Notice how the central character keeps waking up to the same life, literally and symbolically, until he stops complaining and resisting as he eventually turns toward the only moments he has -- the present. As he comes closer and closer to touching and embracing this now, a transformation occurs. He wakes up.

There you have it, a very few suggestions for touring the world of mindfulness in various forms. There are many more. Follow your nose and you are sure to find your sweet spot of inspirations and instruction.

But above all, find a way to put mindfulness to practice. As Yogi Bera supposedly said, "In theory, there is no difference between theory and practice. In practice, there is." Mindfulness awaits you with the turn of your head. It awaits you in the next breath fully and consciously experienced. It smiles in the midst of your emotional storms. It pulls up a chair wondering if you will invite it to dinner, to a time with a friend, or to a sunset.

About the Author

Martin Lumpkin holds a PhD in clinical psychology. He currently practices psychotherapy and teaches graduate students as a part-time professor at the University of Texas Southwestern Medical Center in Dallas. His passion is teaching and coaching others in mindfulness.

He lives a lovely life with his wife, Janet, in Terrell, Texas. For more about the author, please visit his website at http://www.martinlumpkin.com/.